I0490123

This book belongs to

———————————

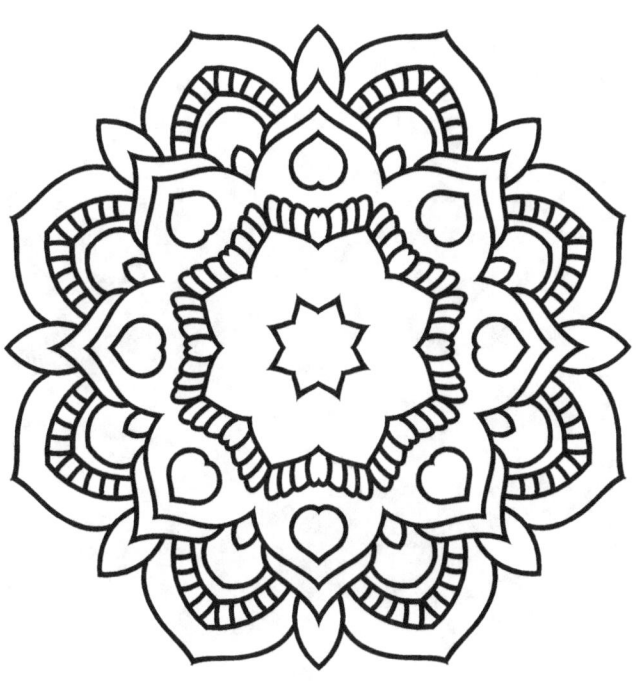

Believe in your intuition.

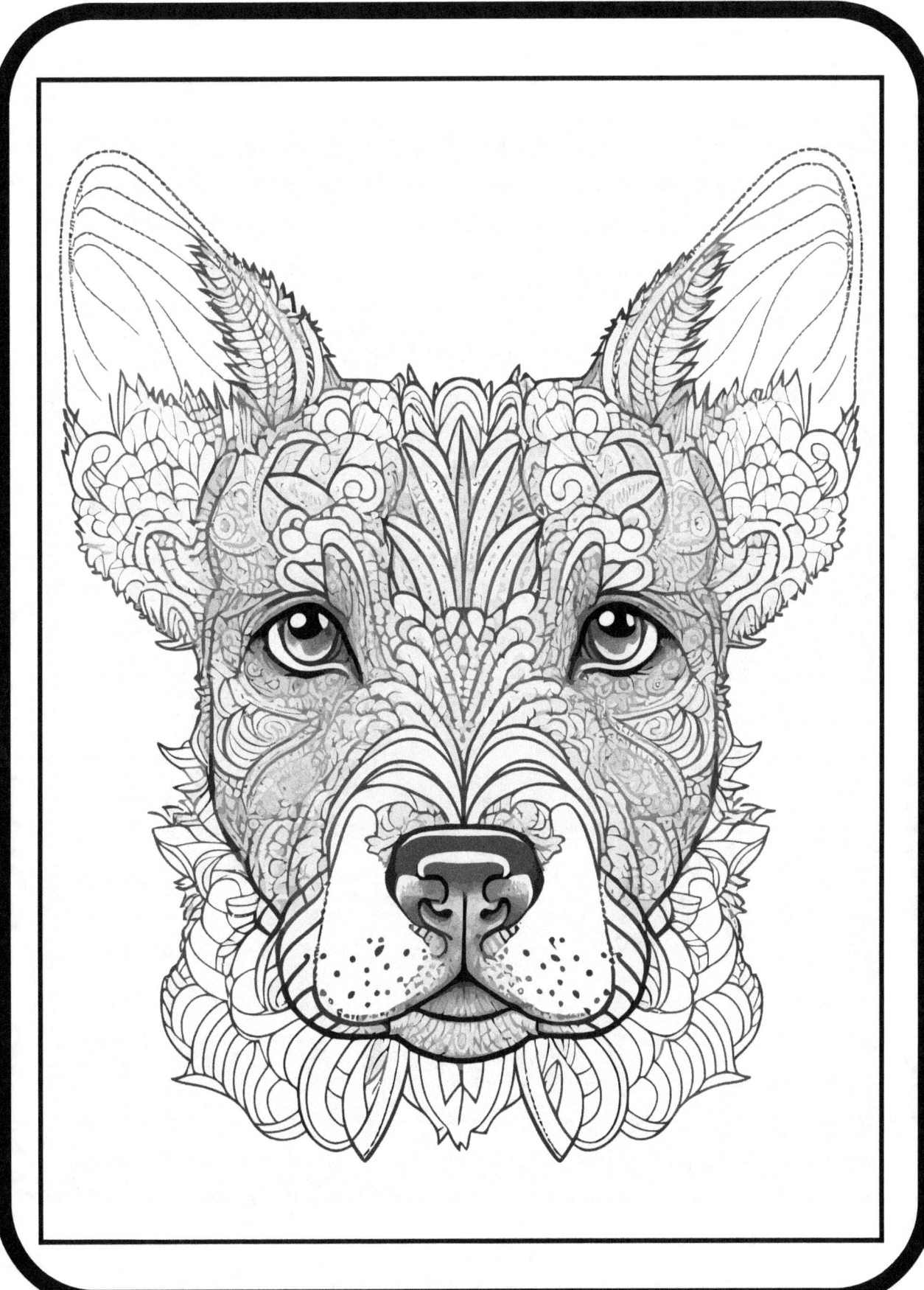

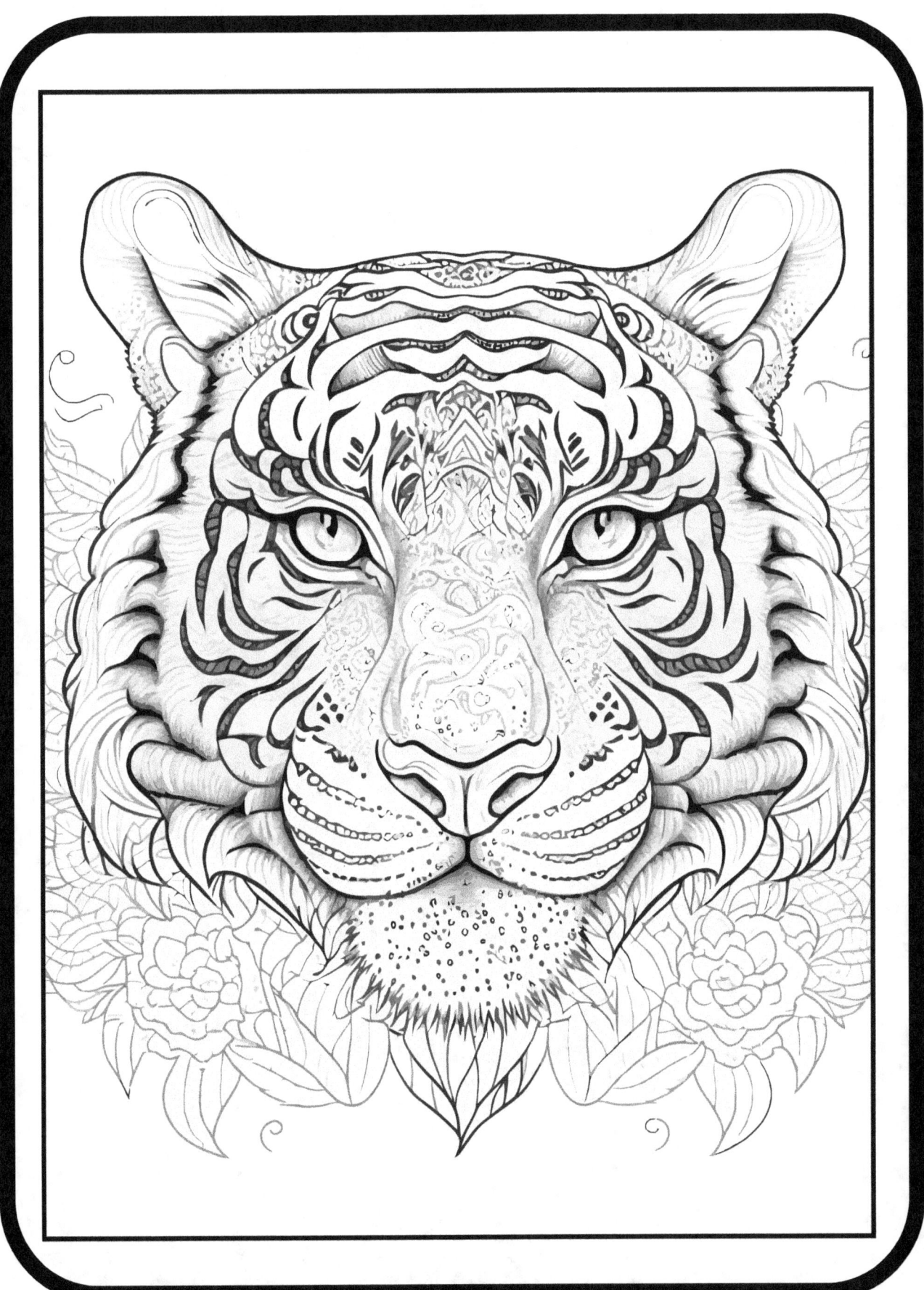

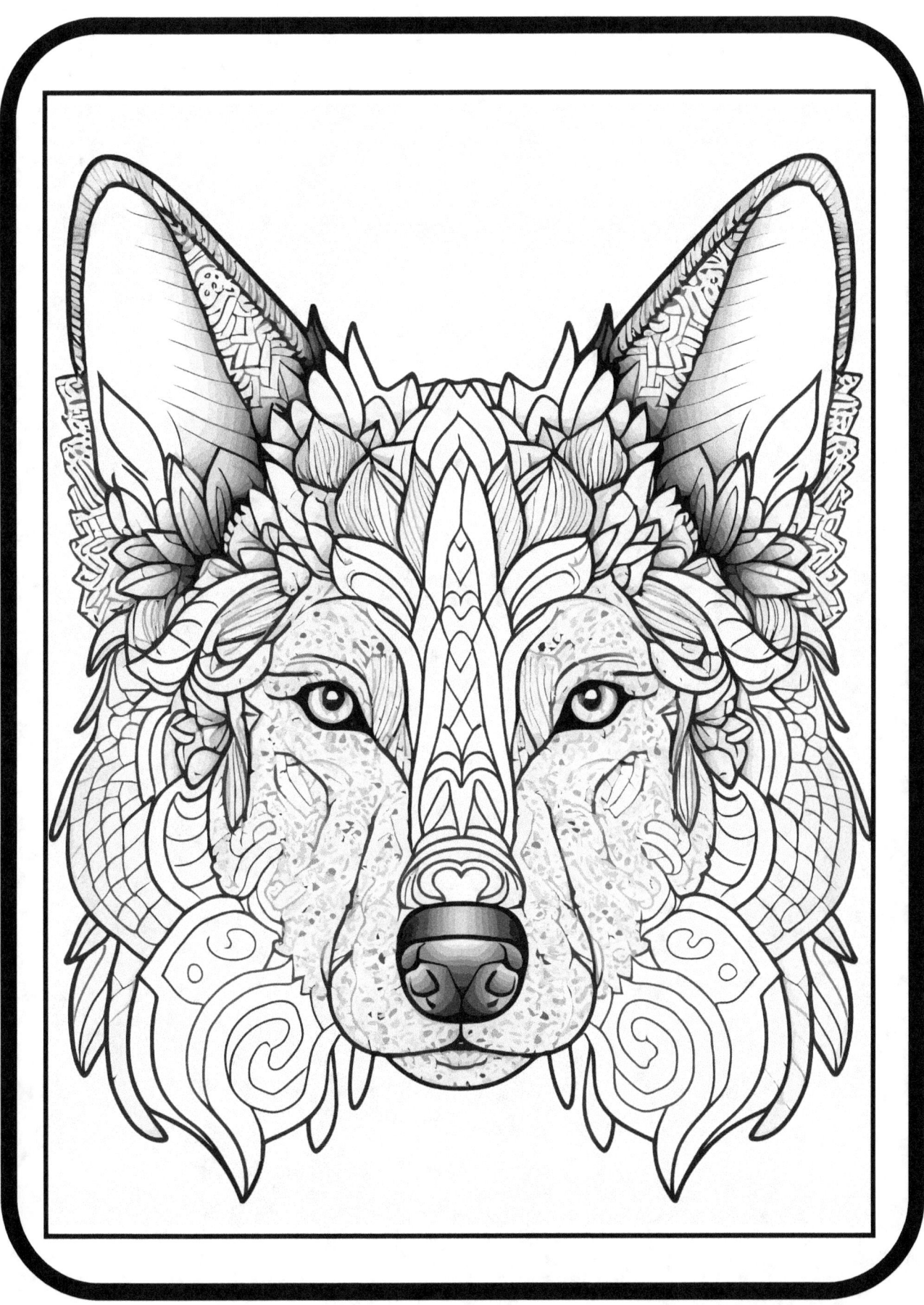

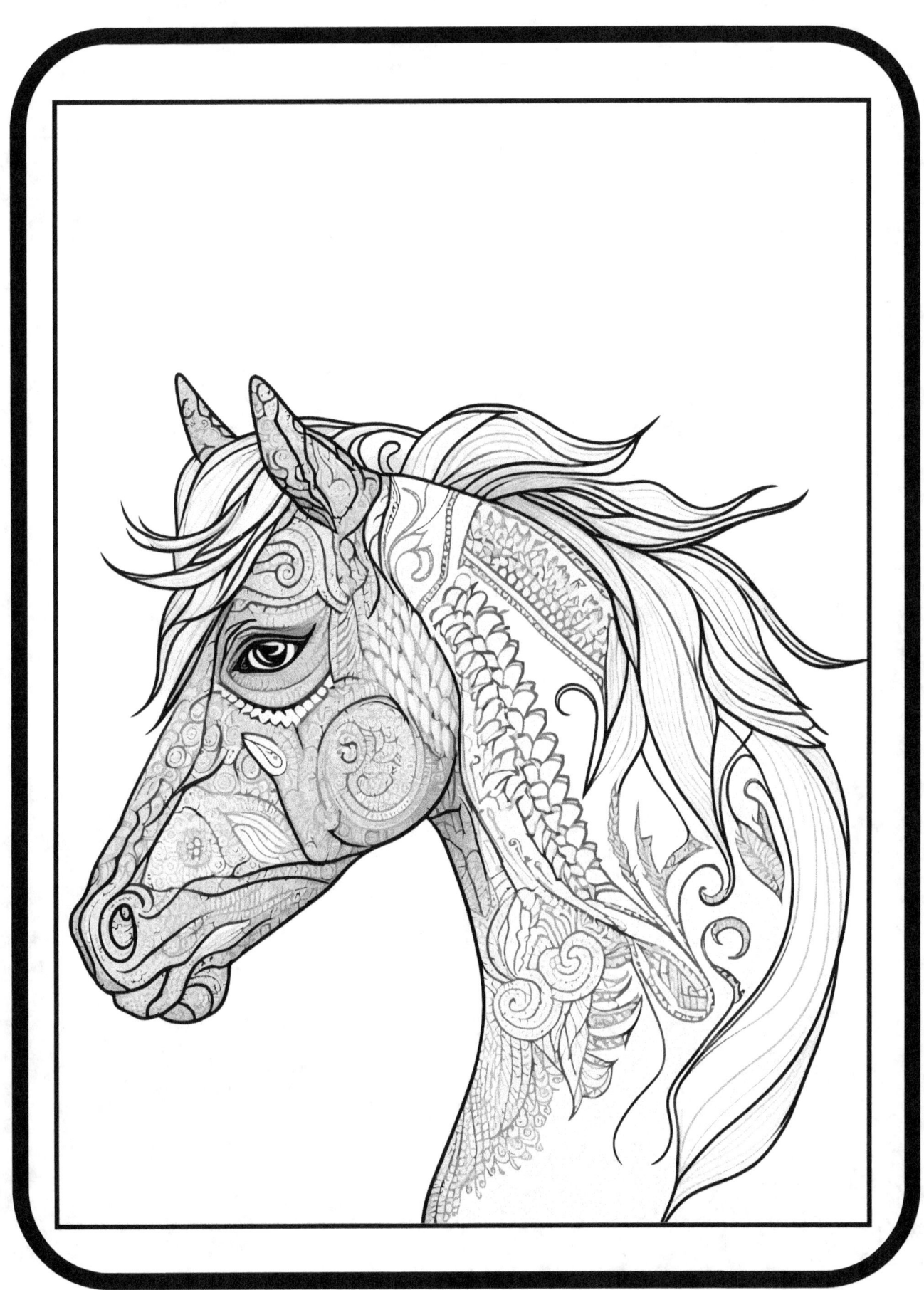

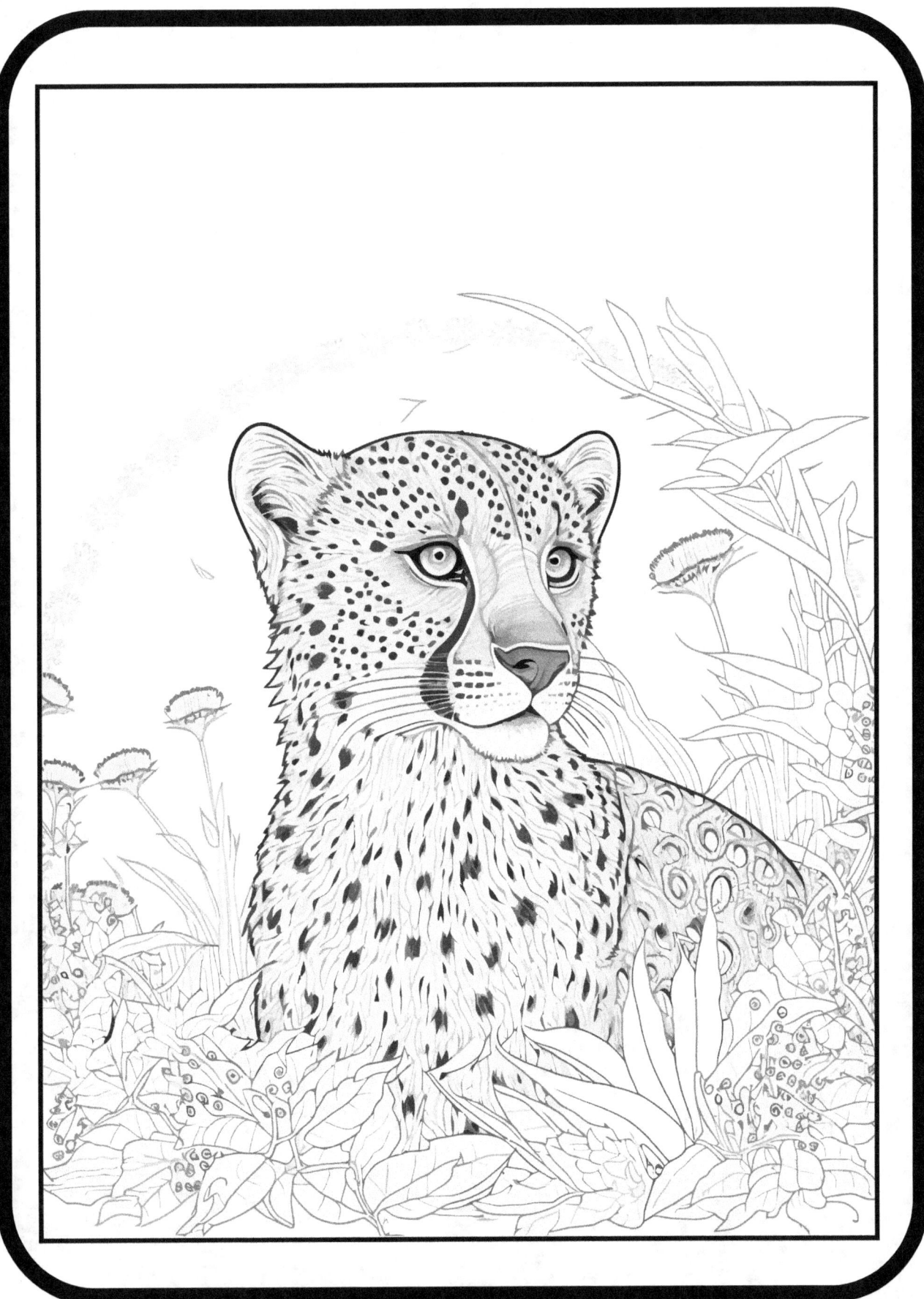

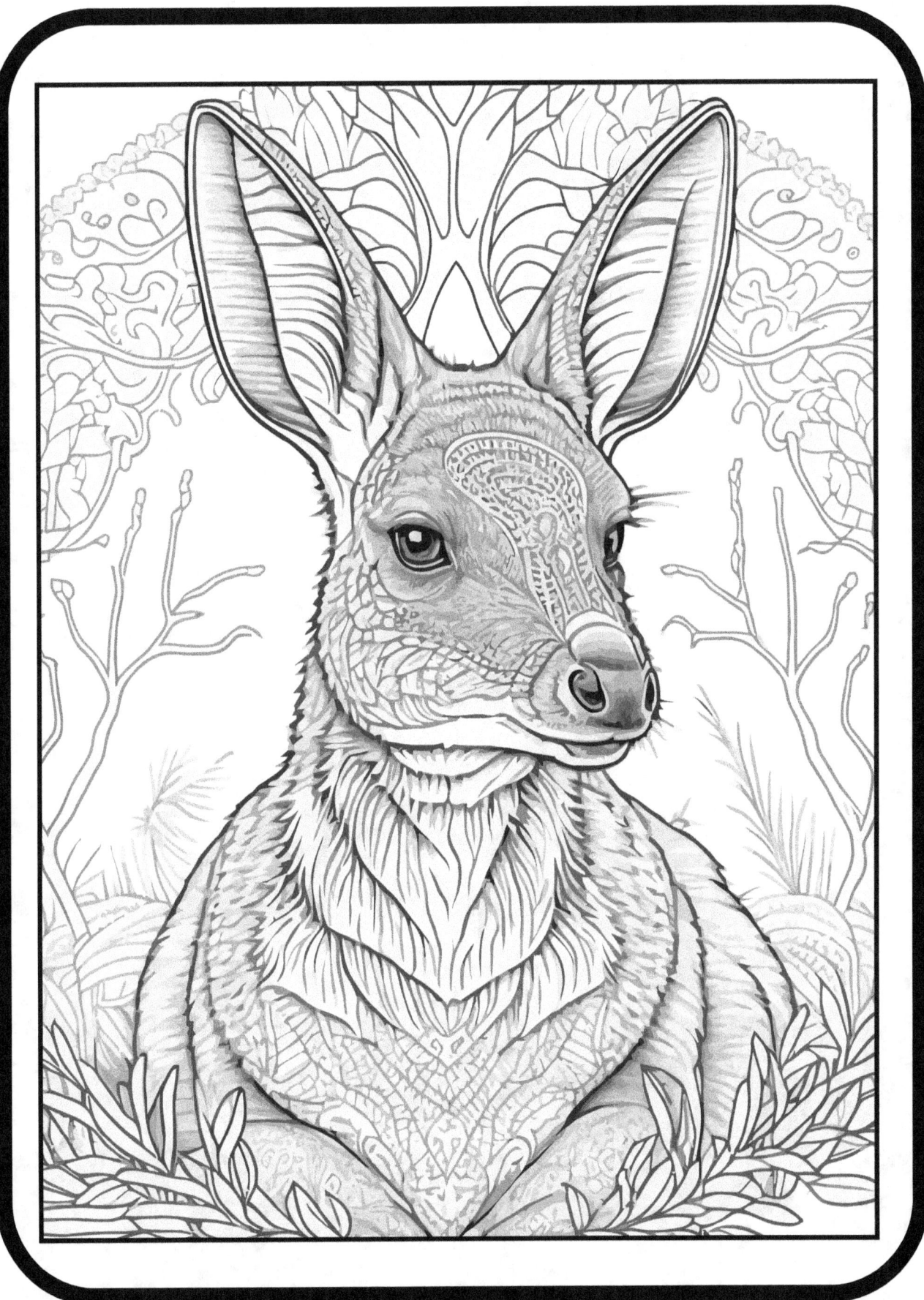

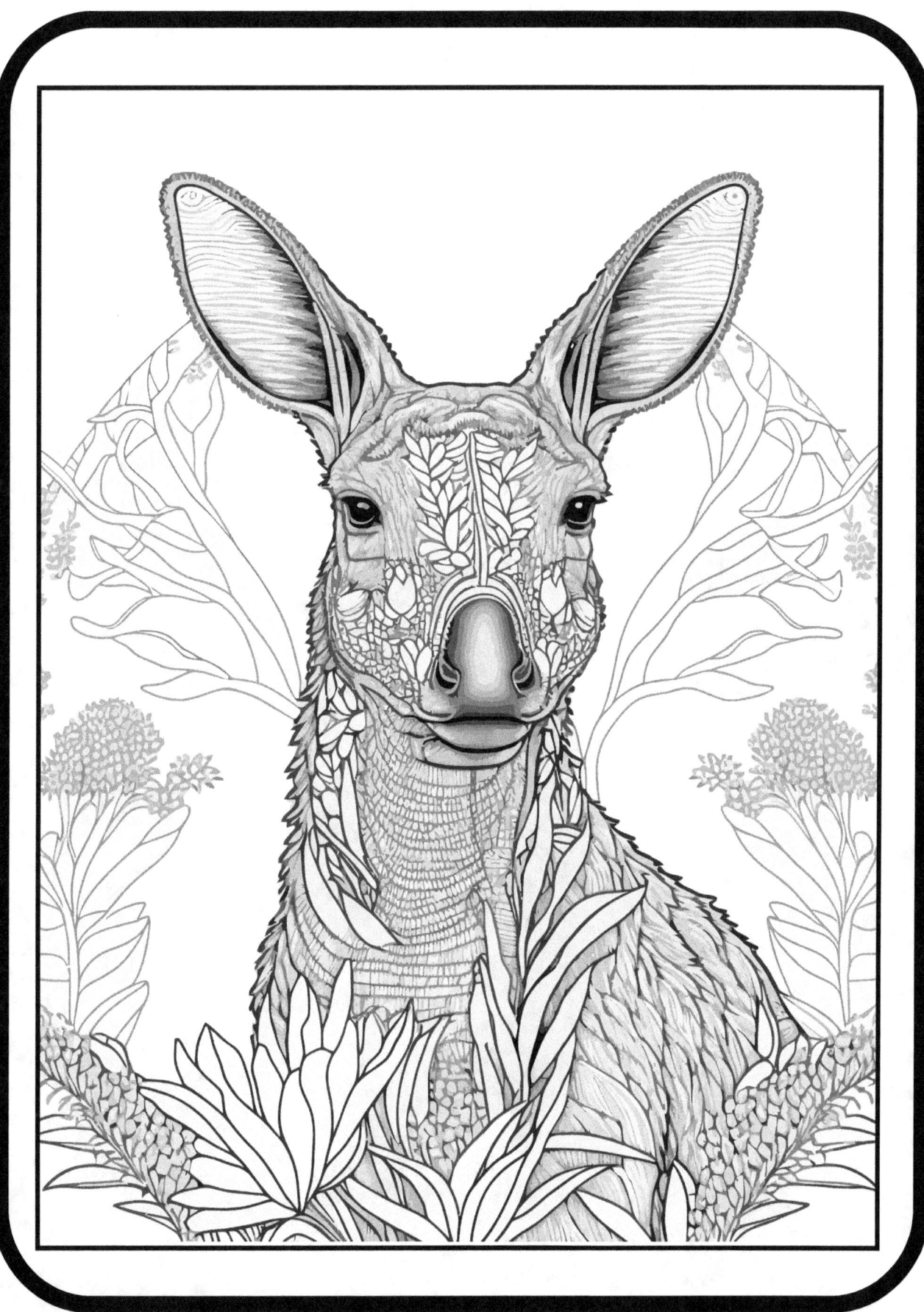

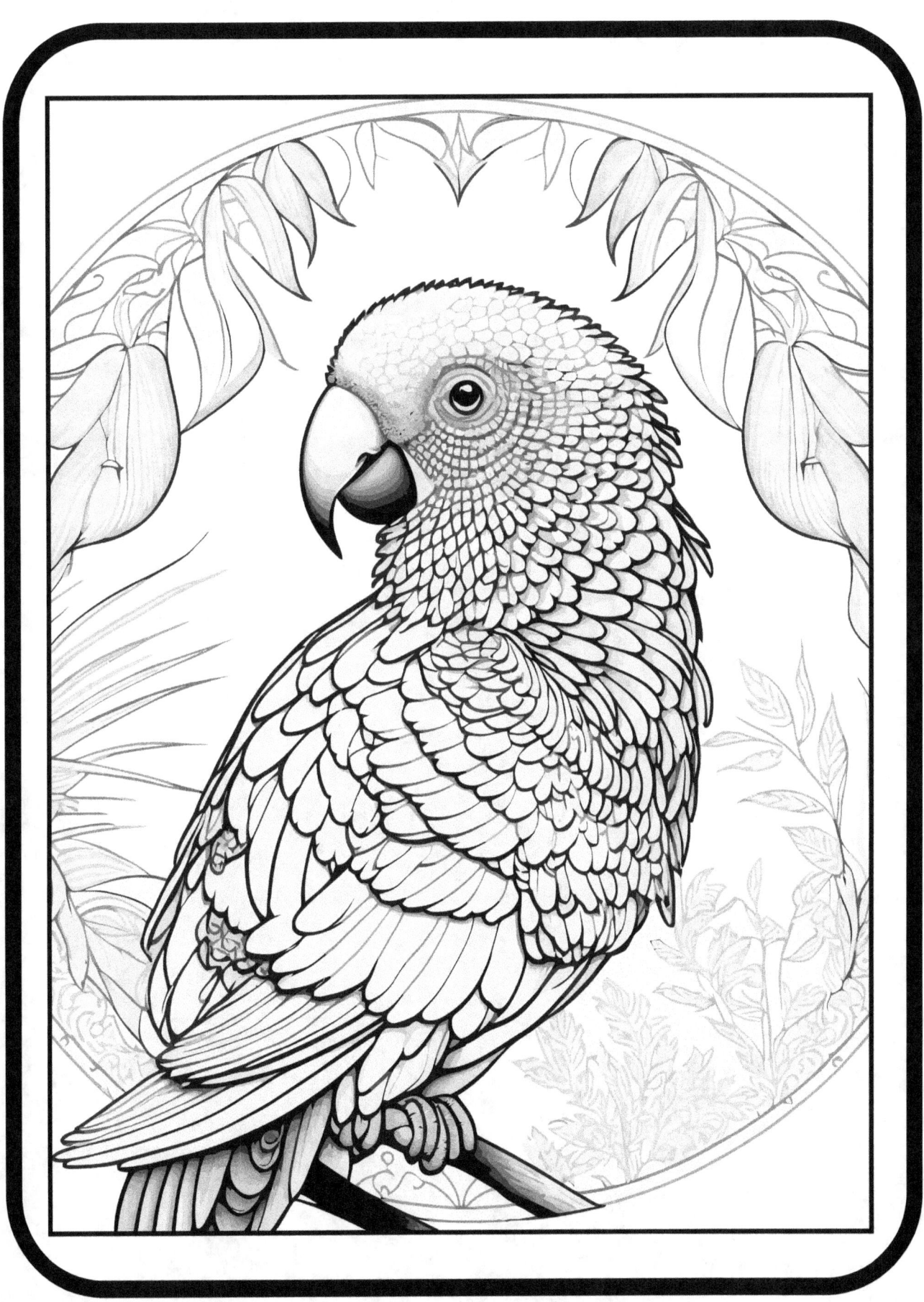

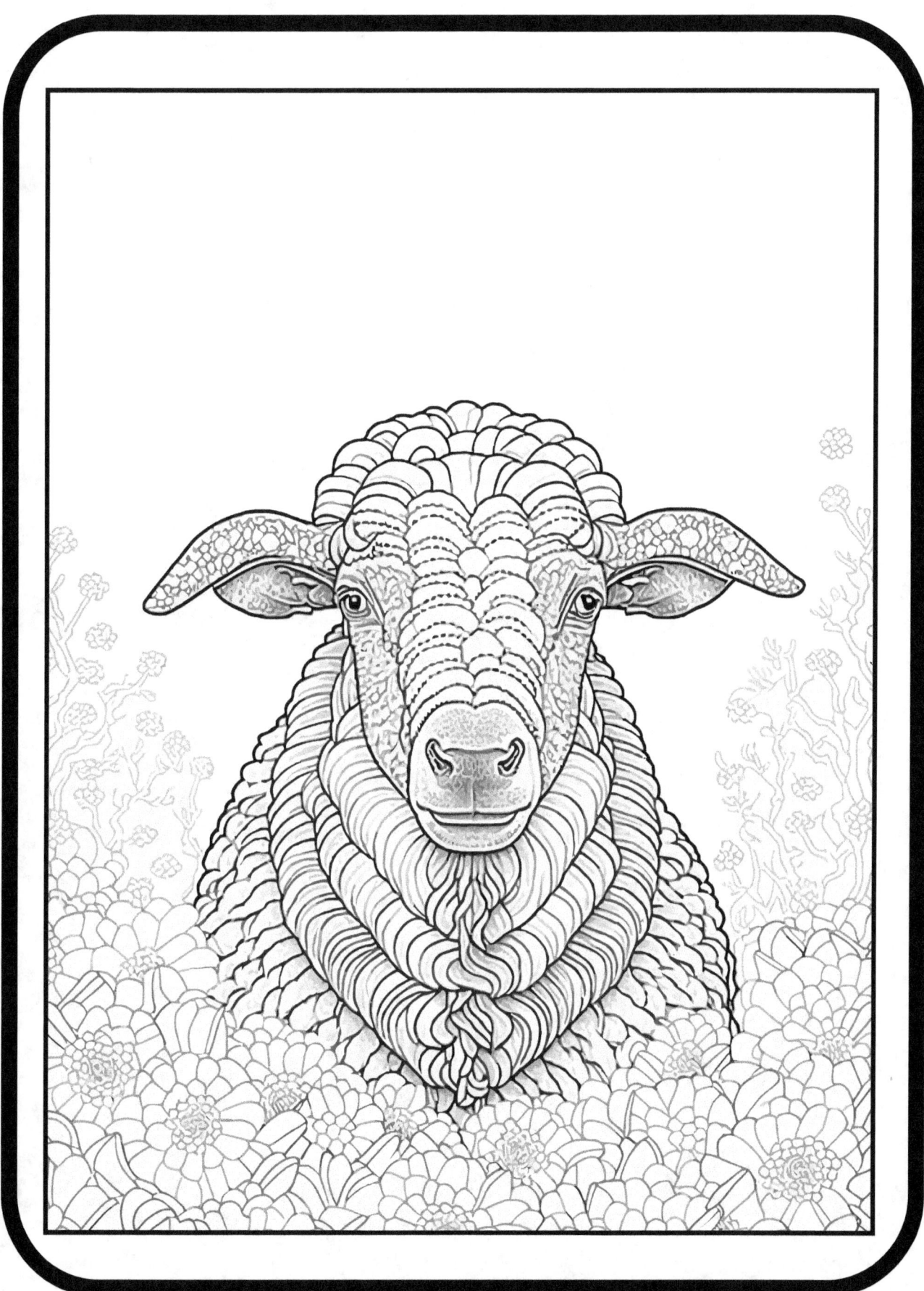

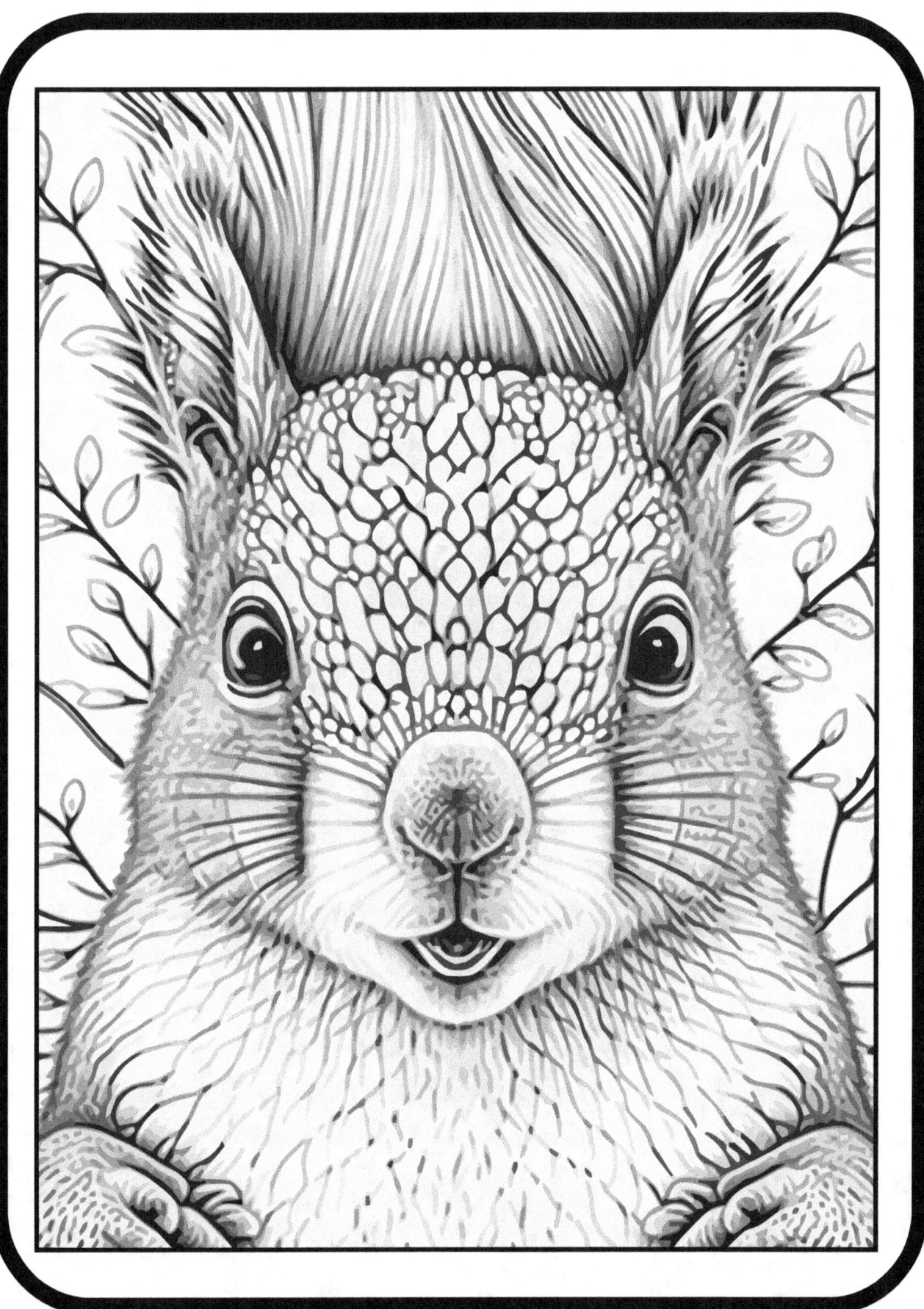

Keep your mindset positive.

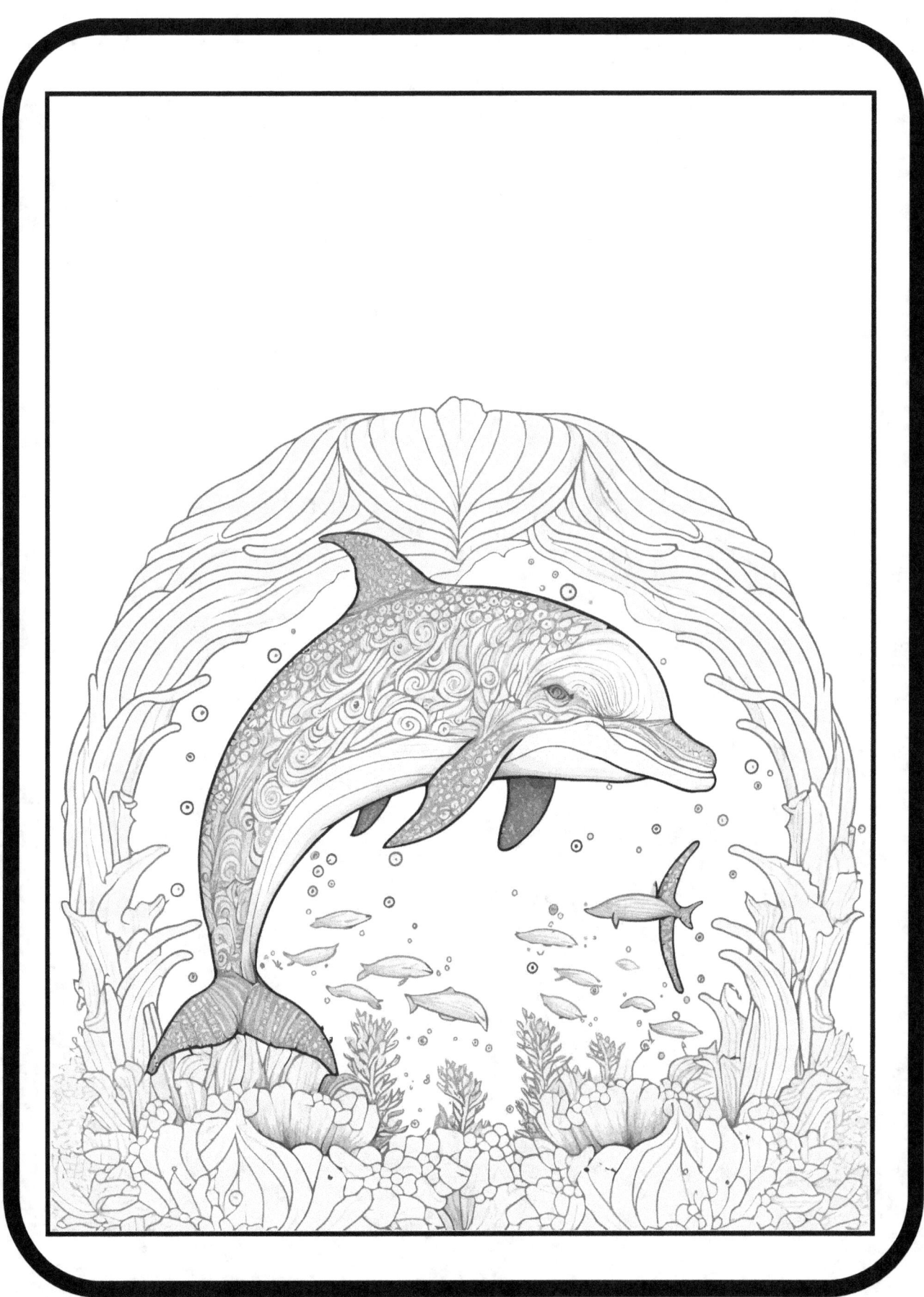

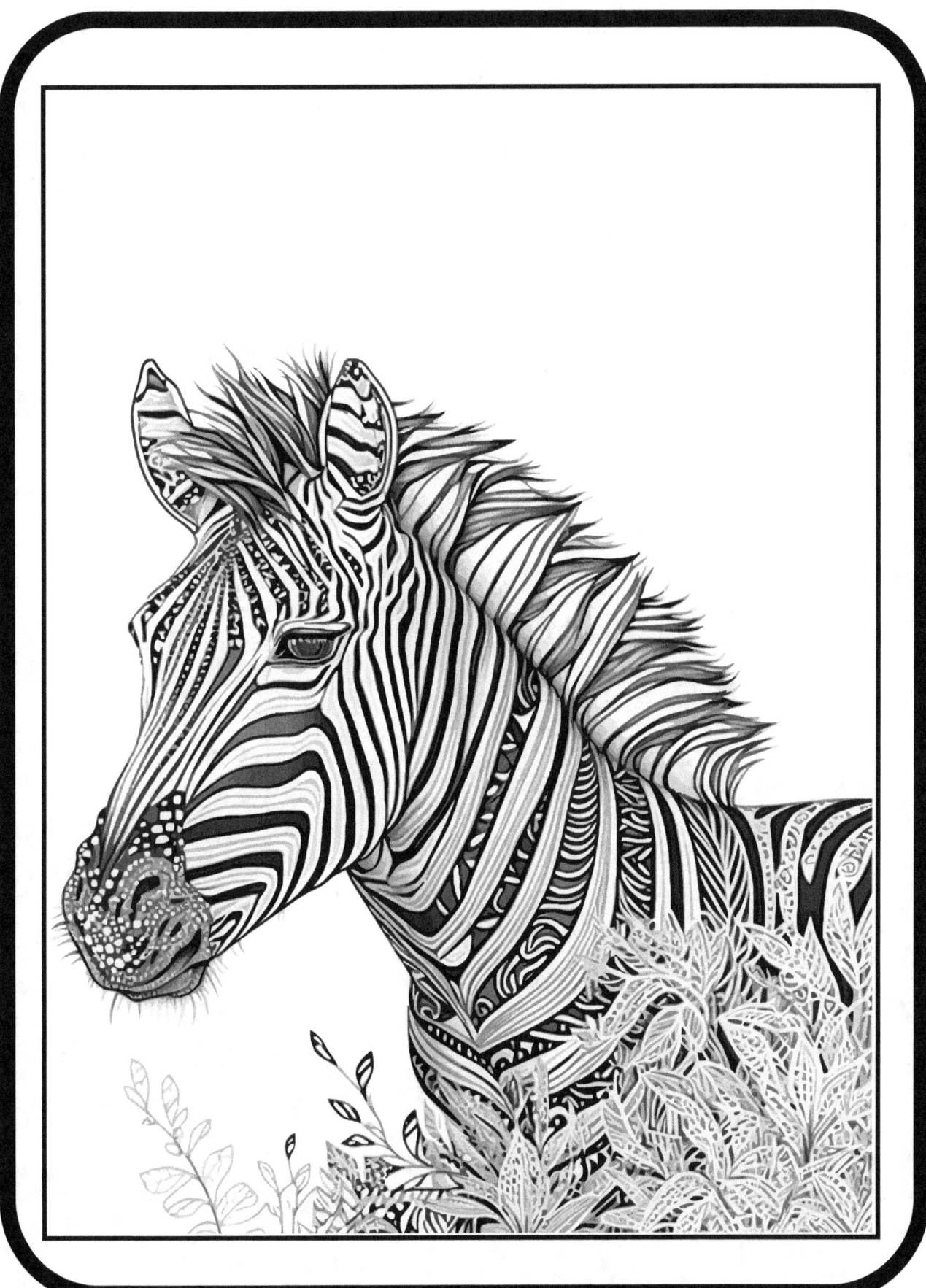

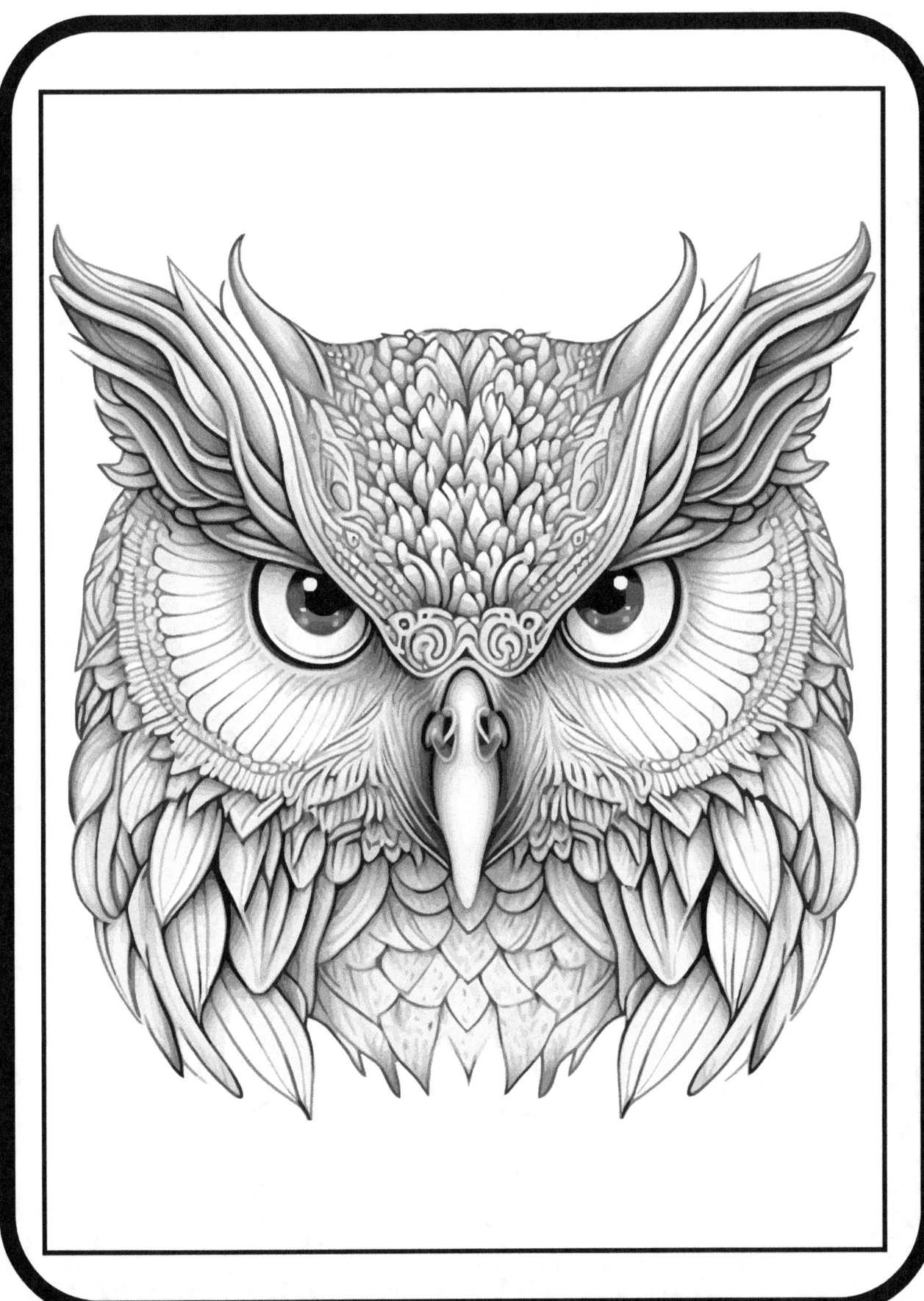

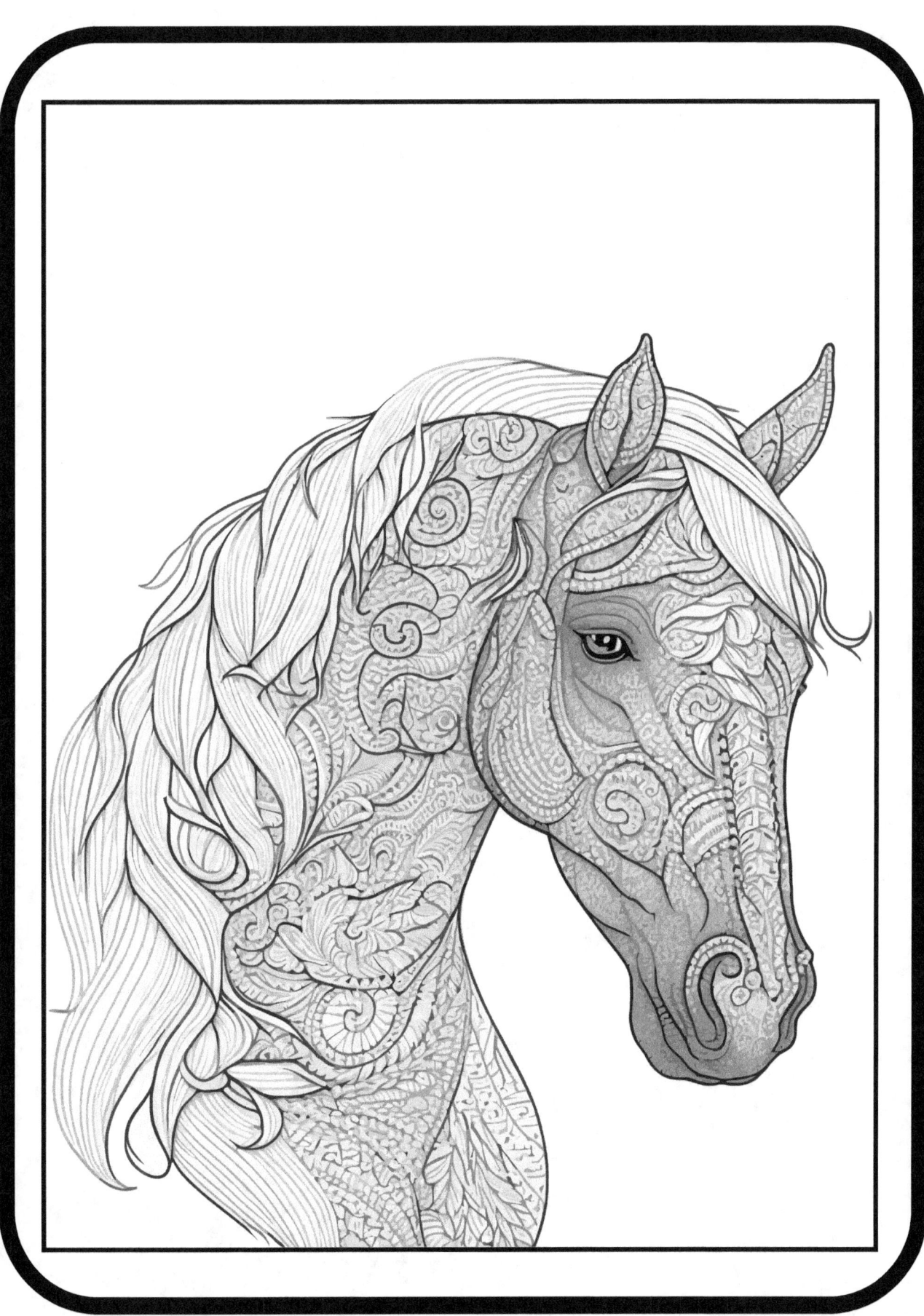

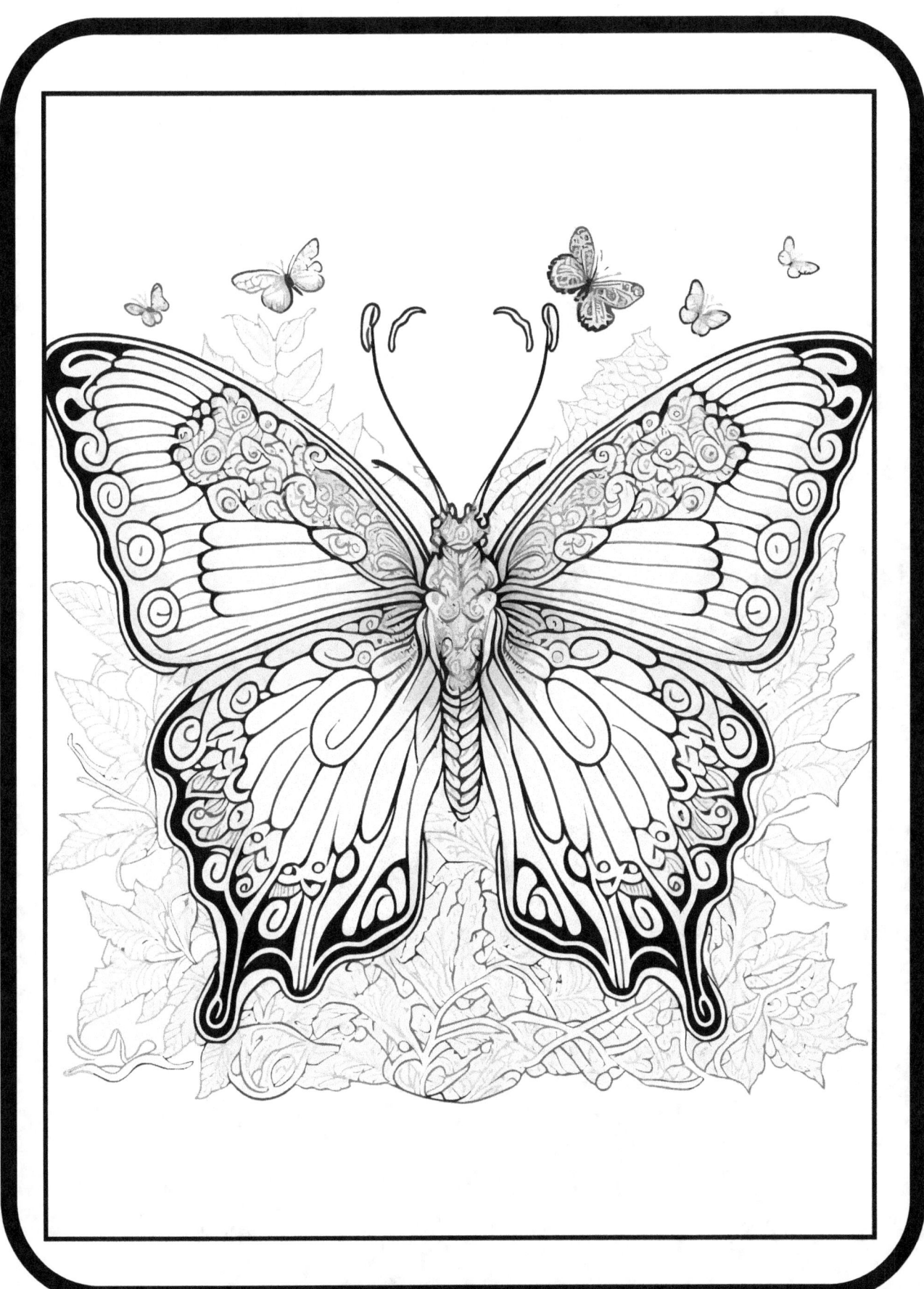

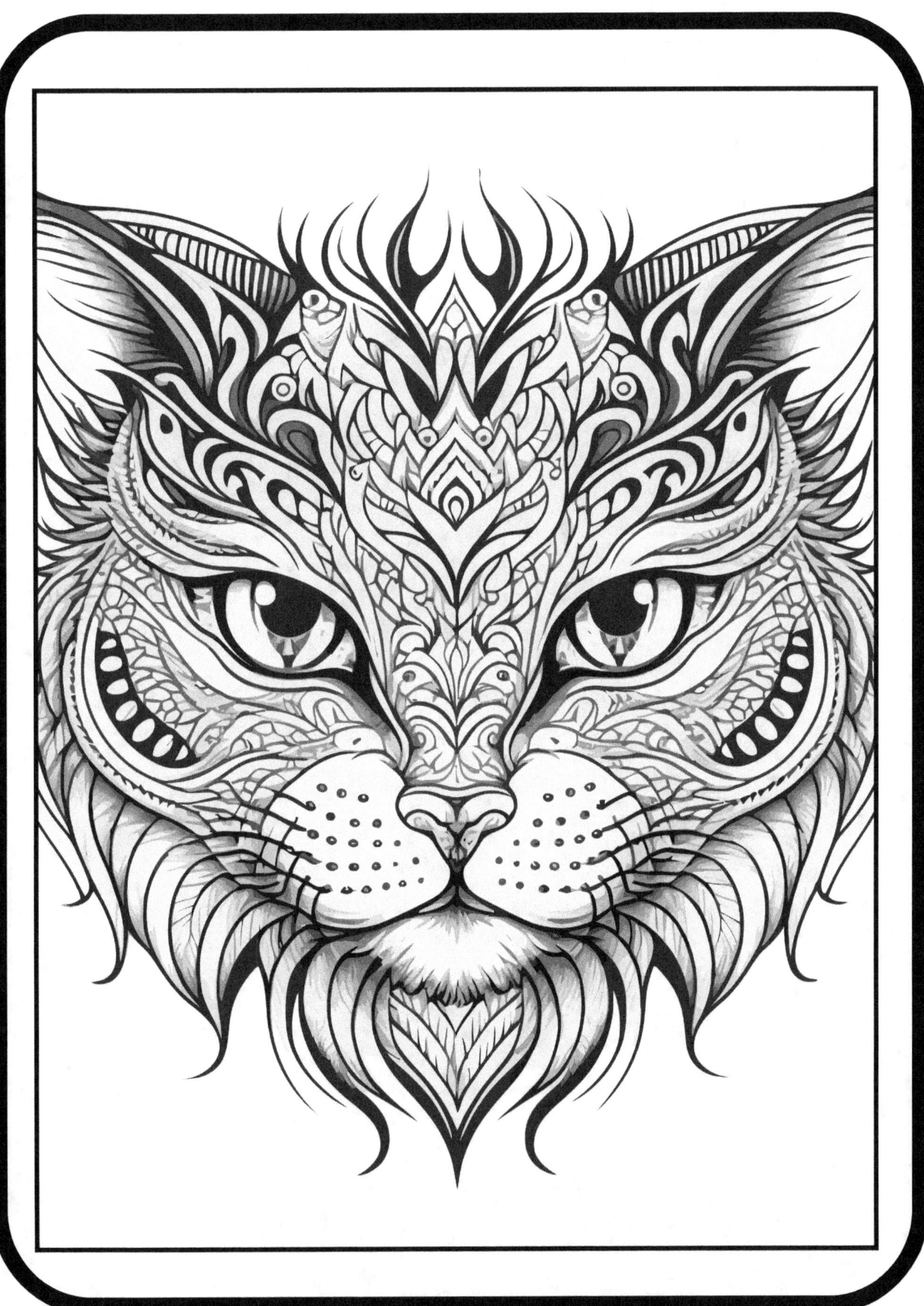

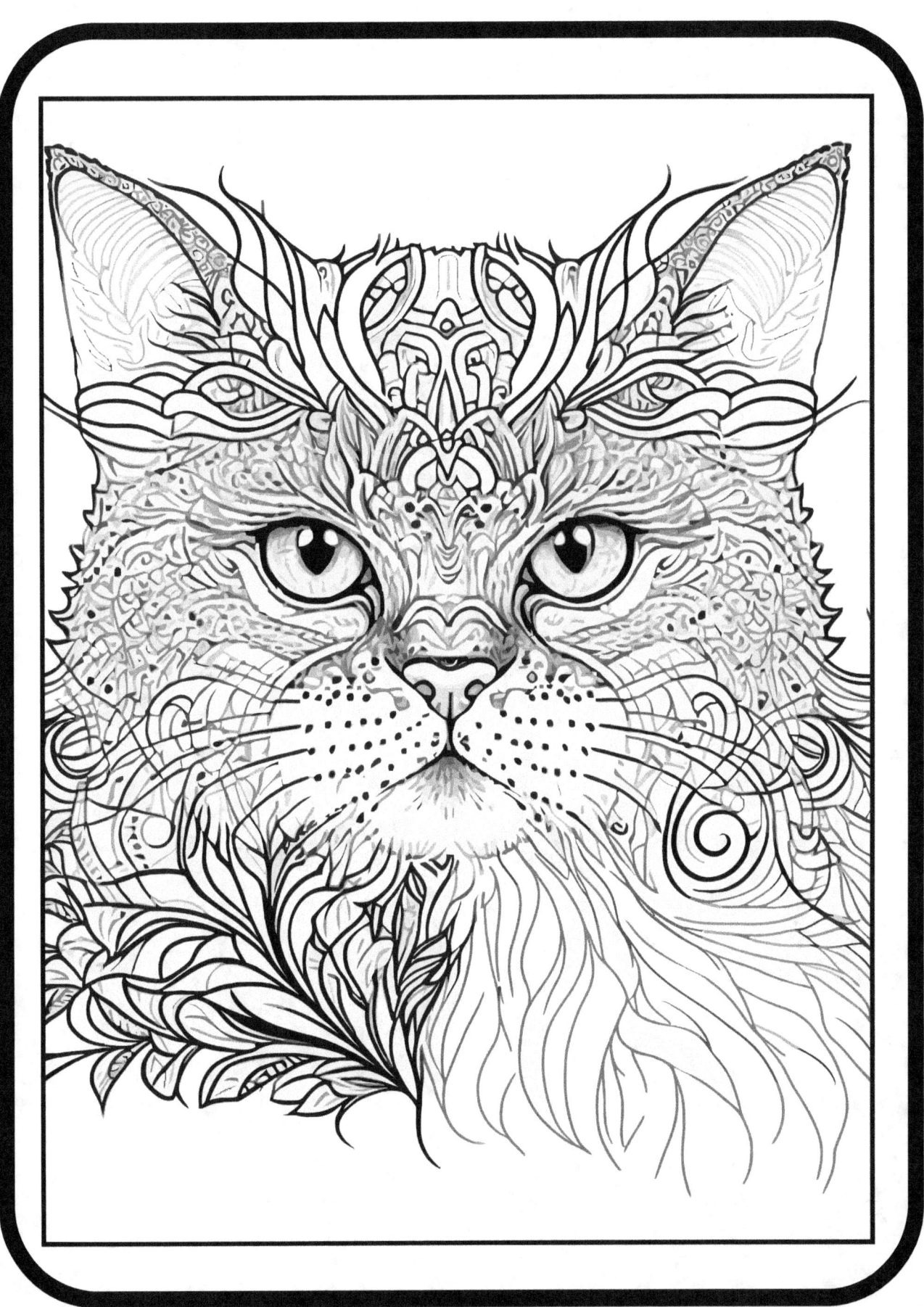

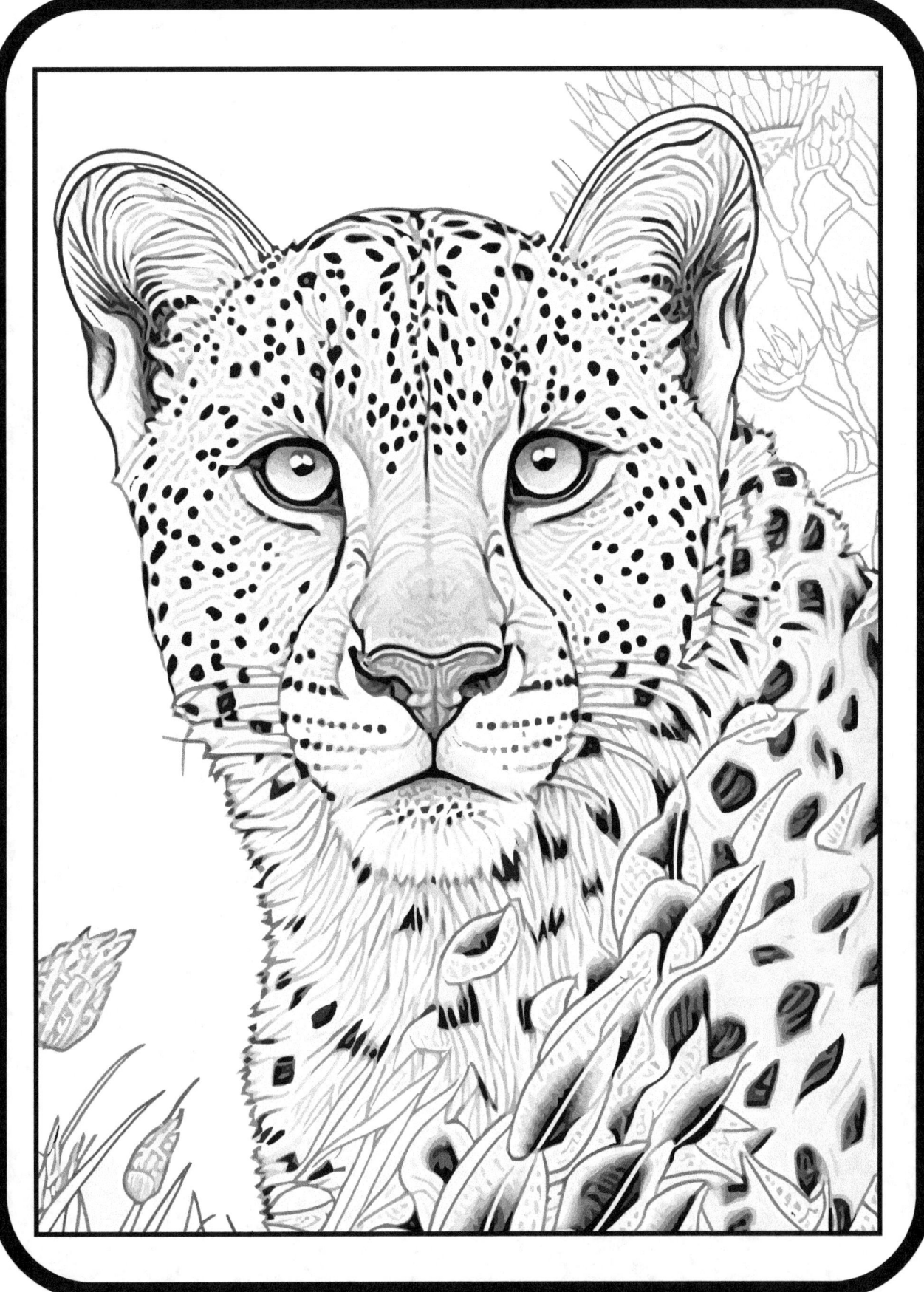

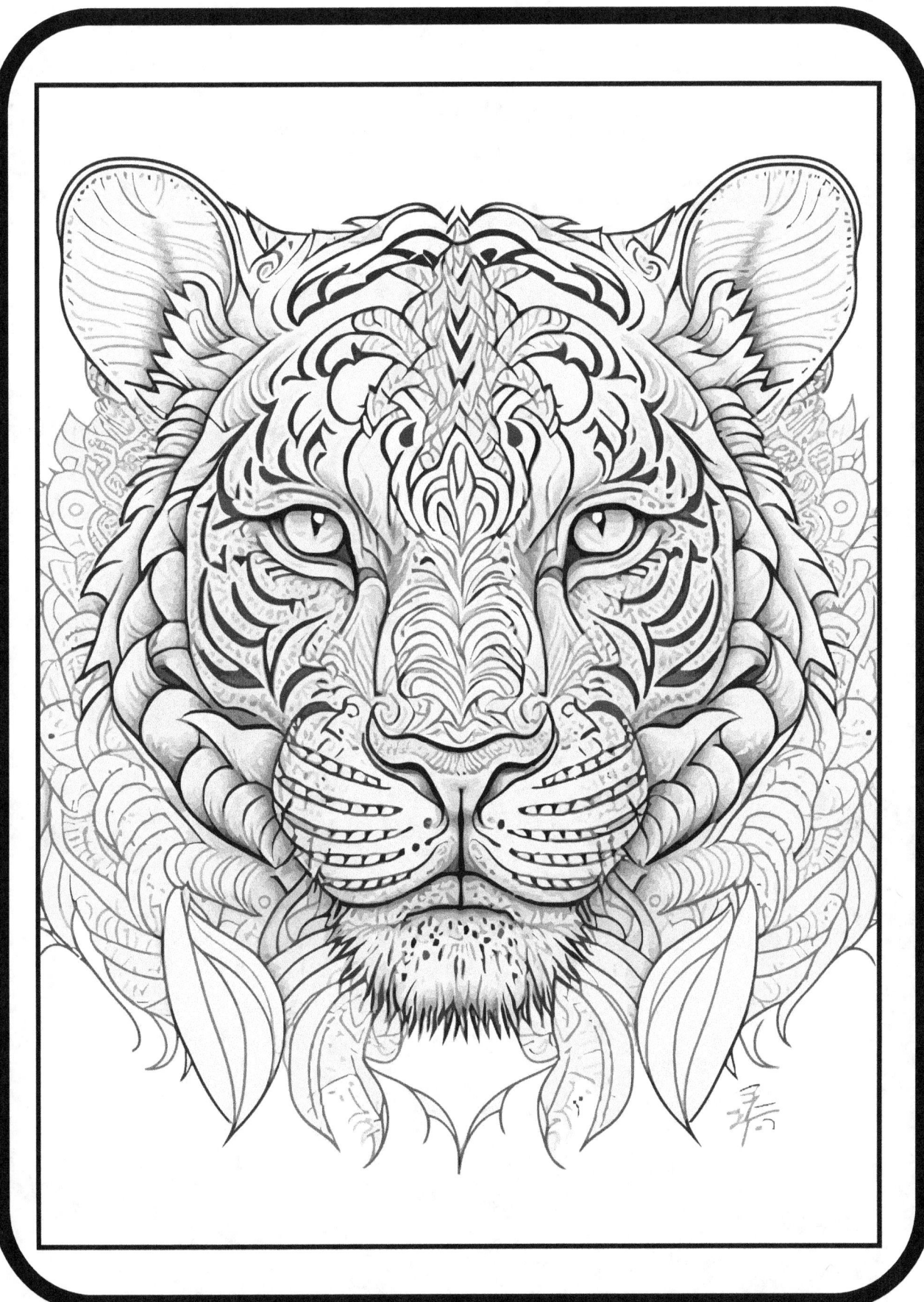

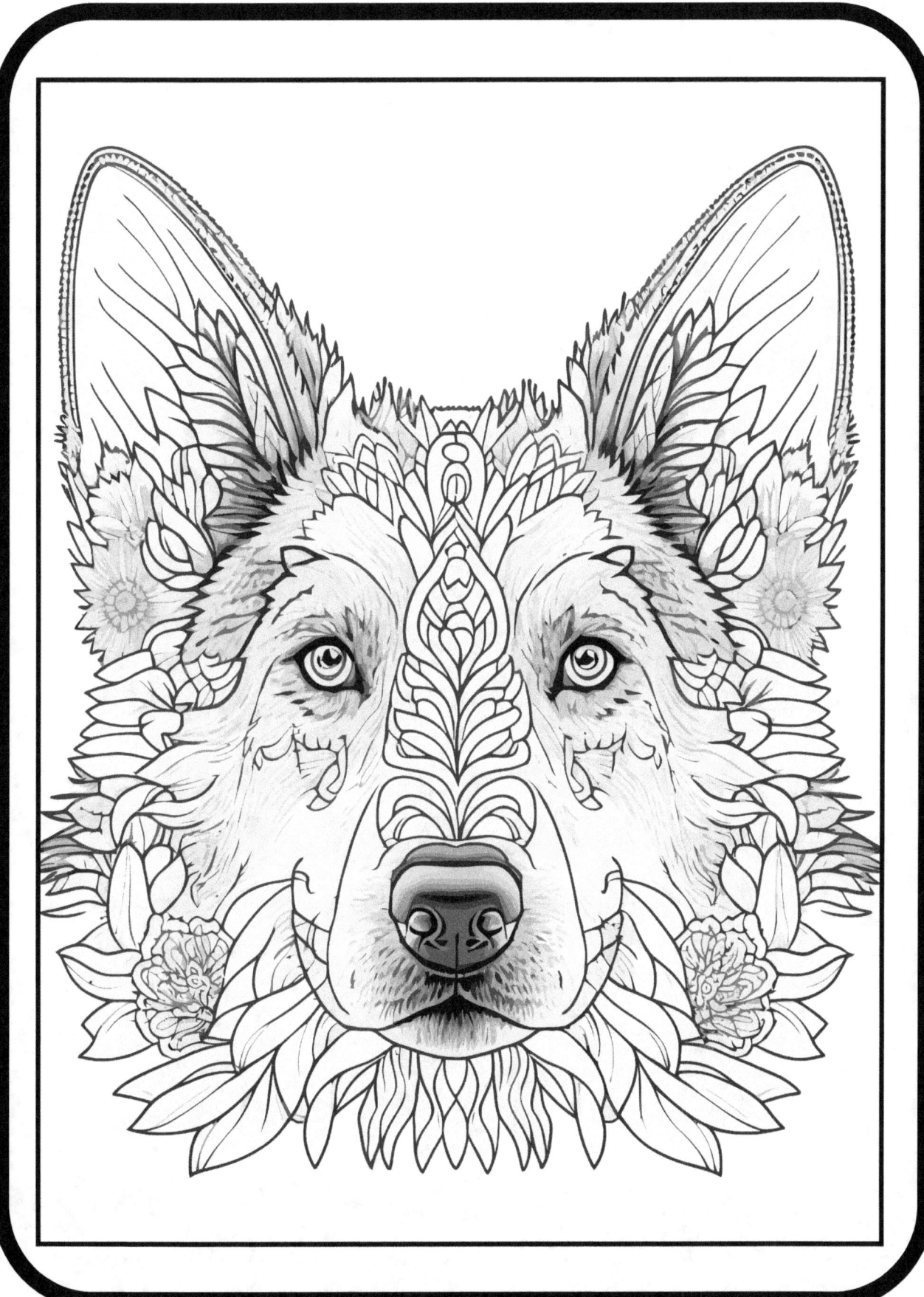

Life is what you make it.

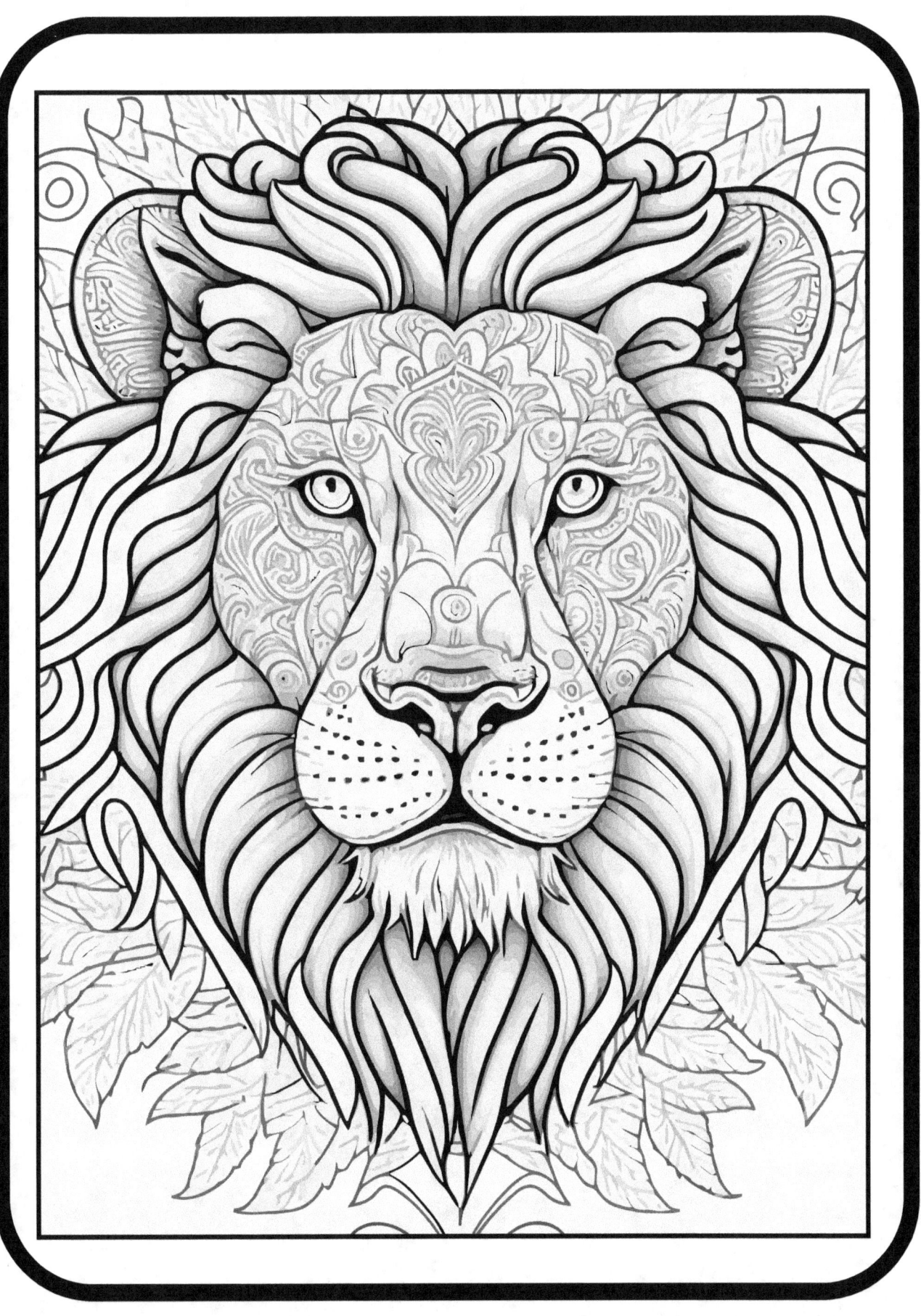

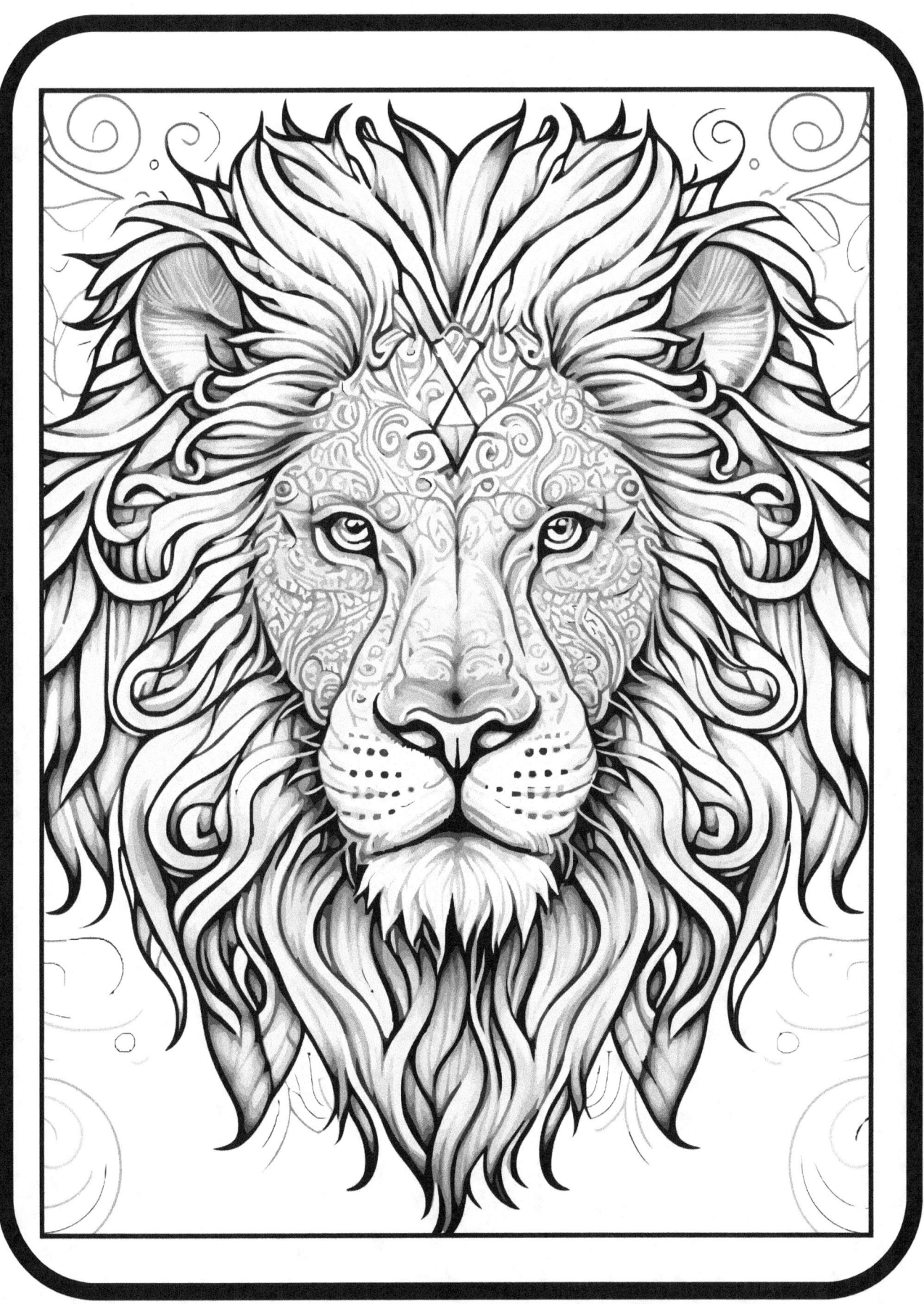

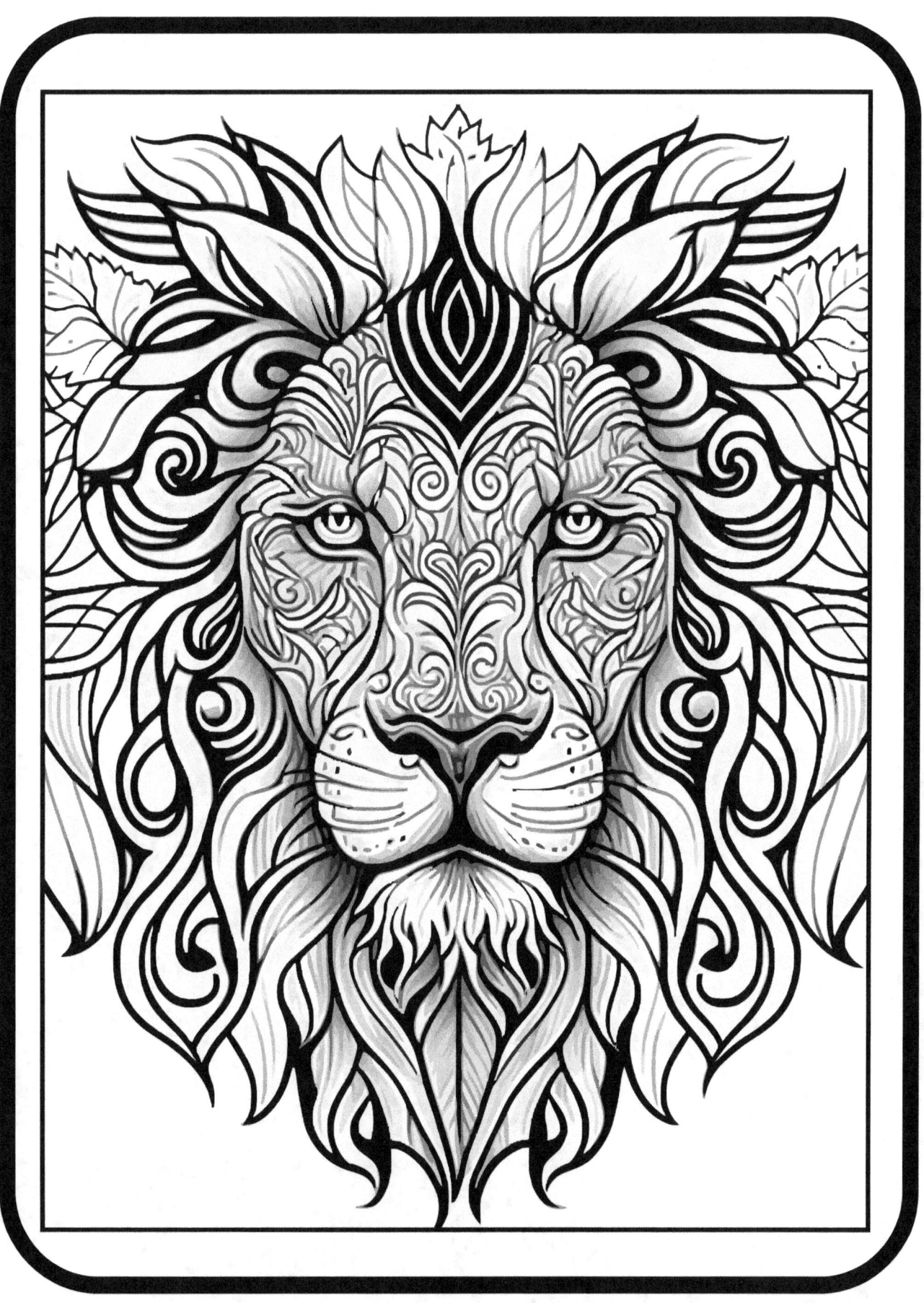

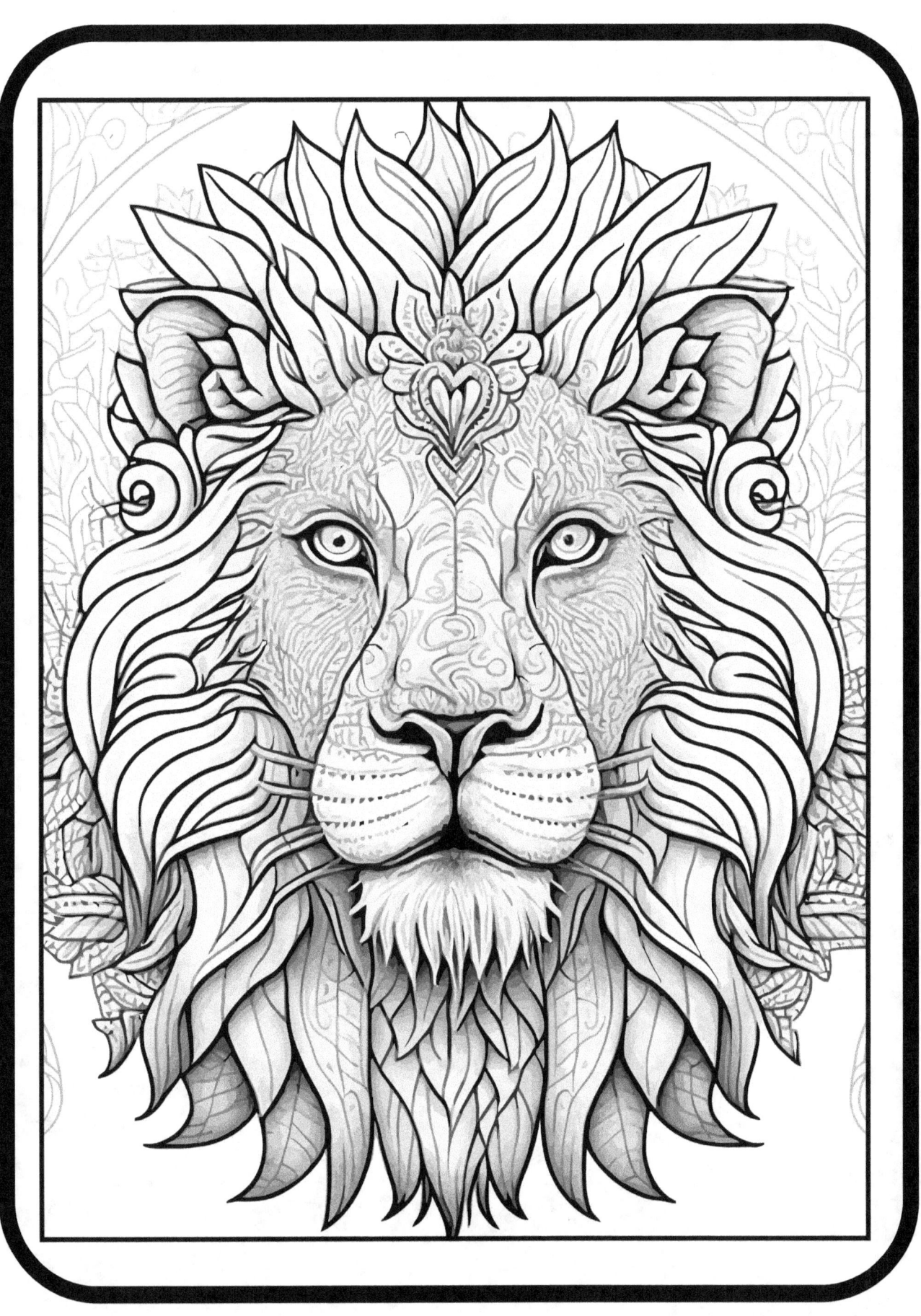

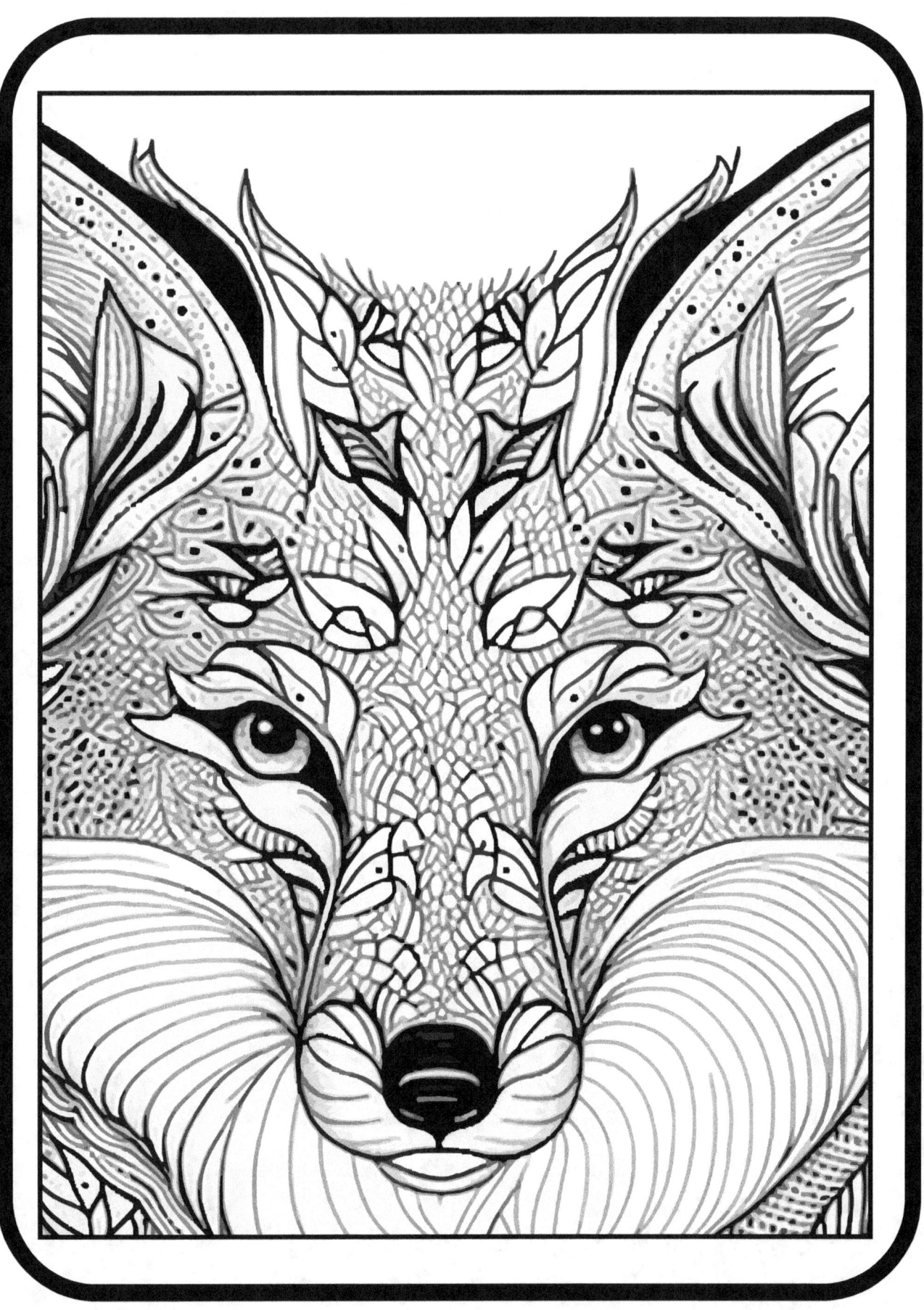

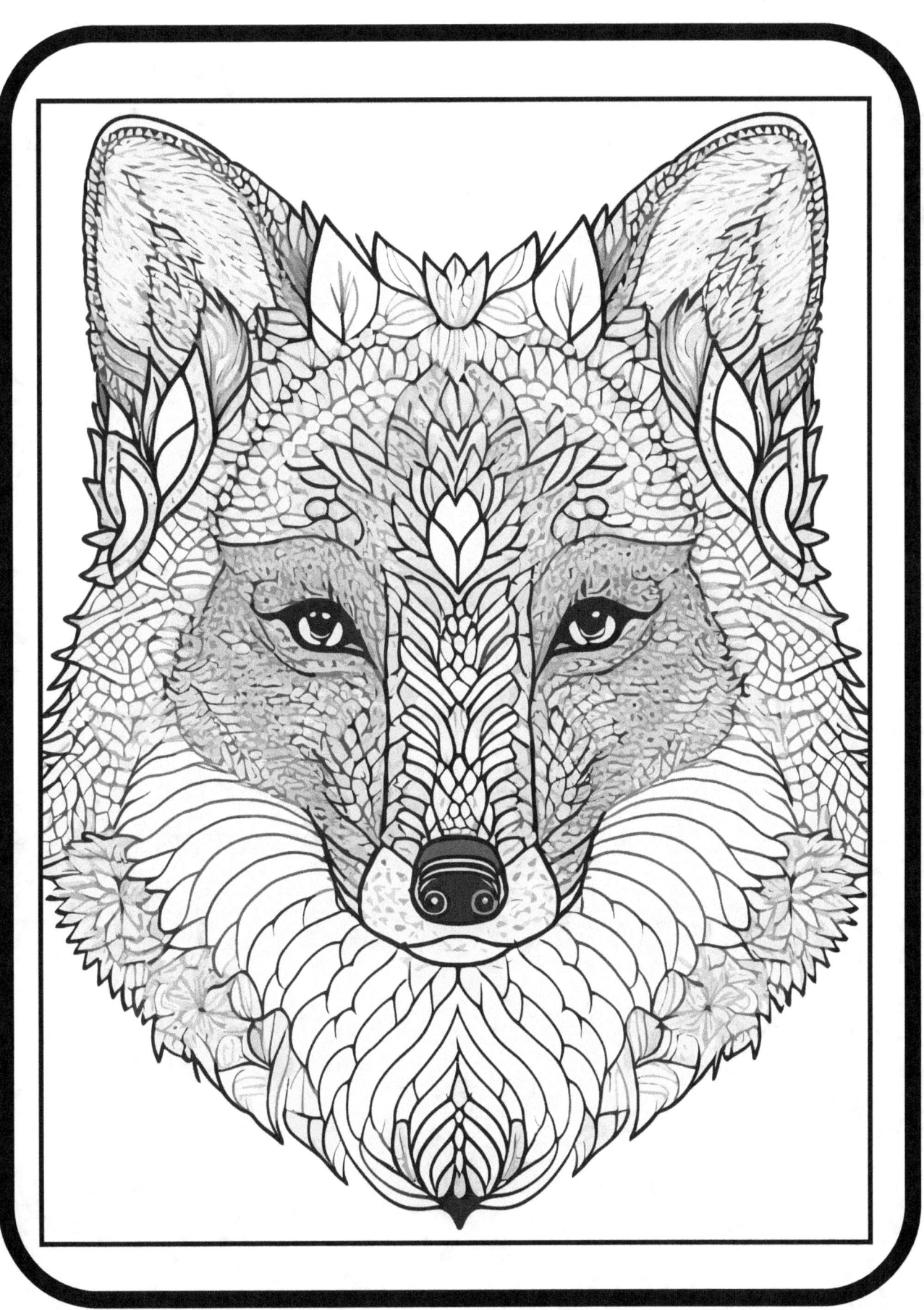

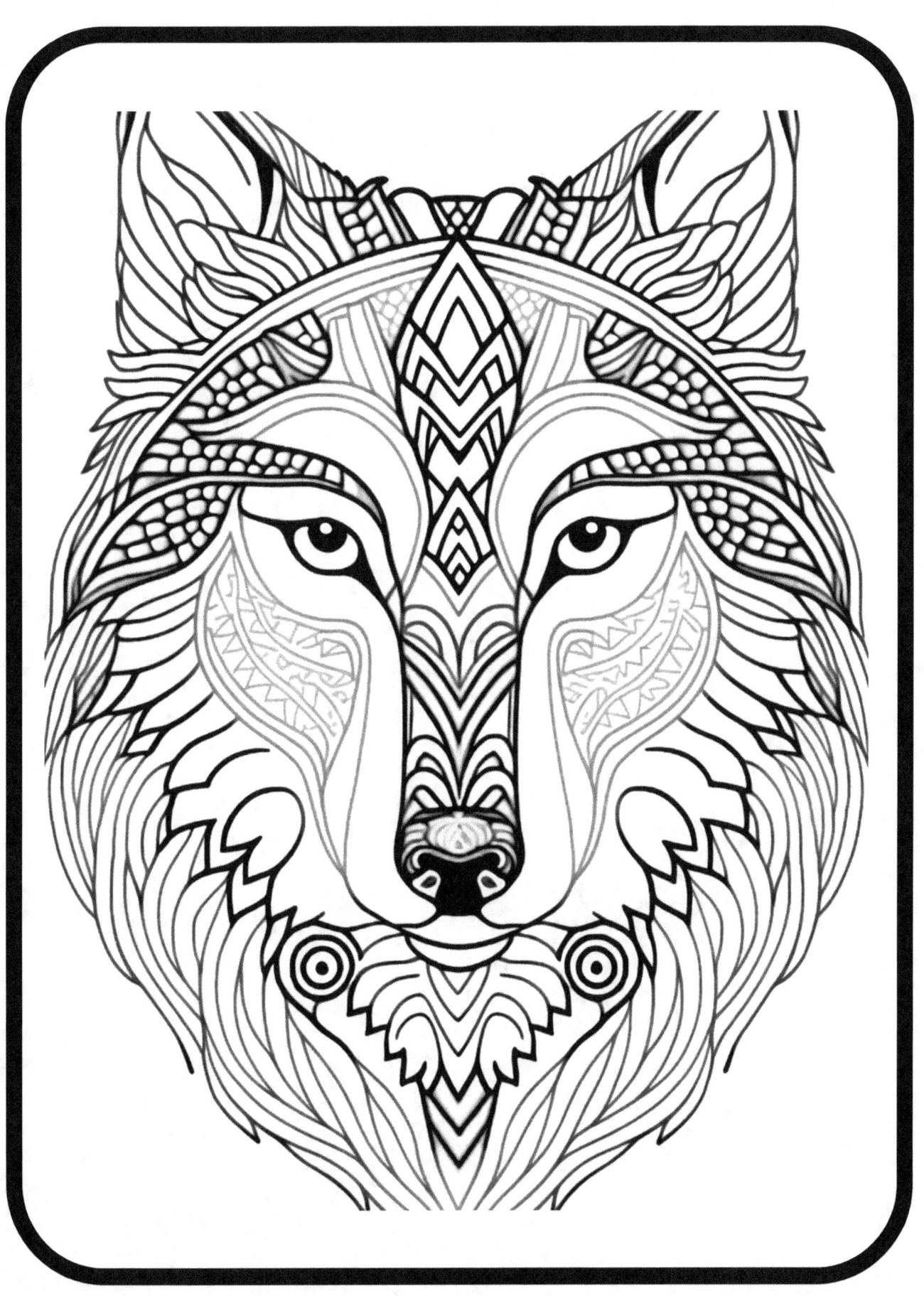

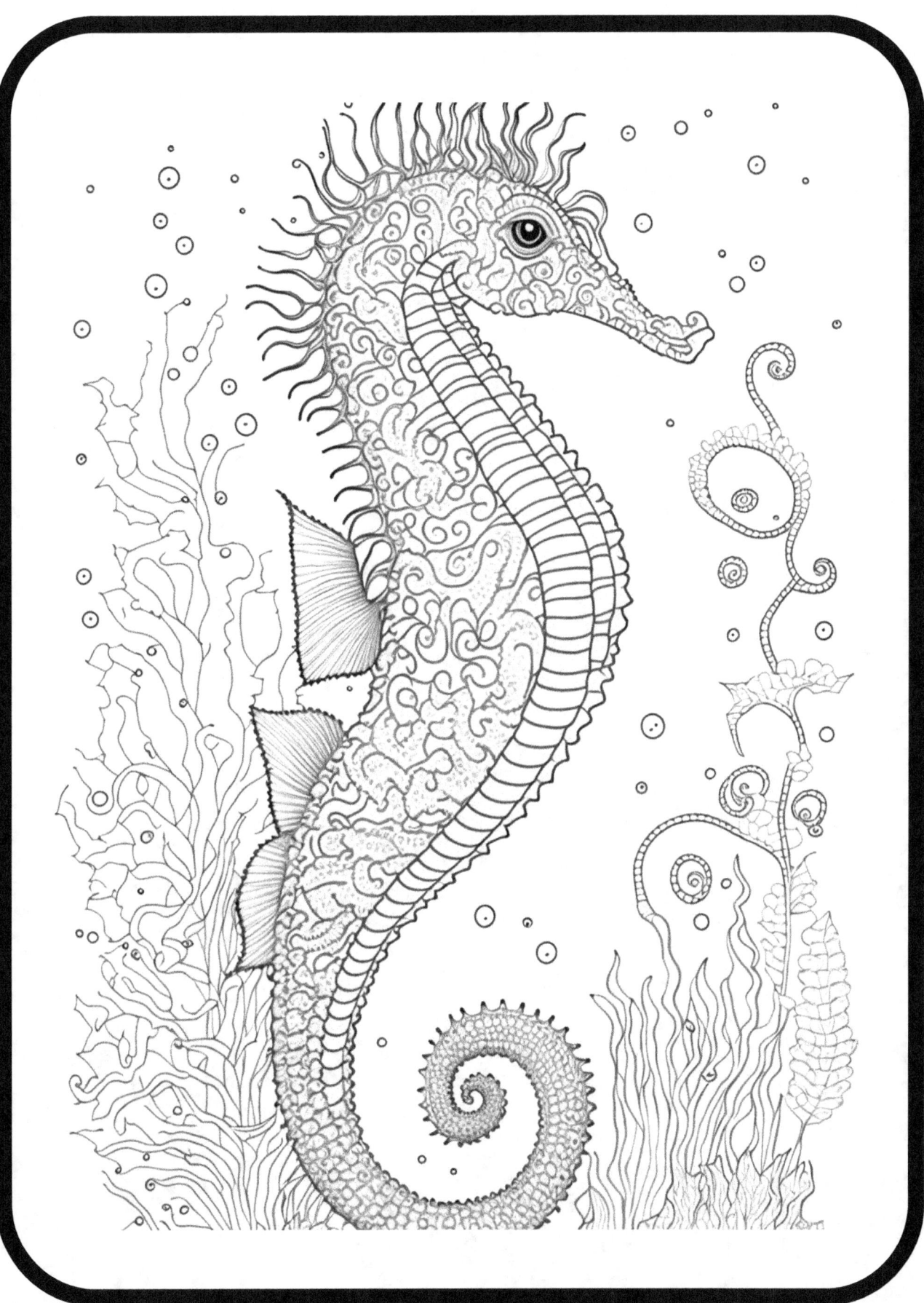

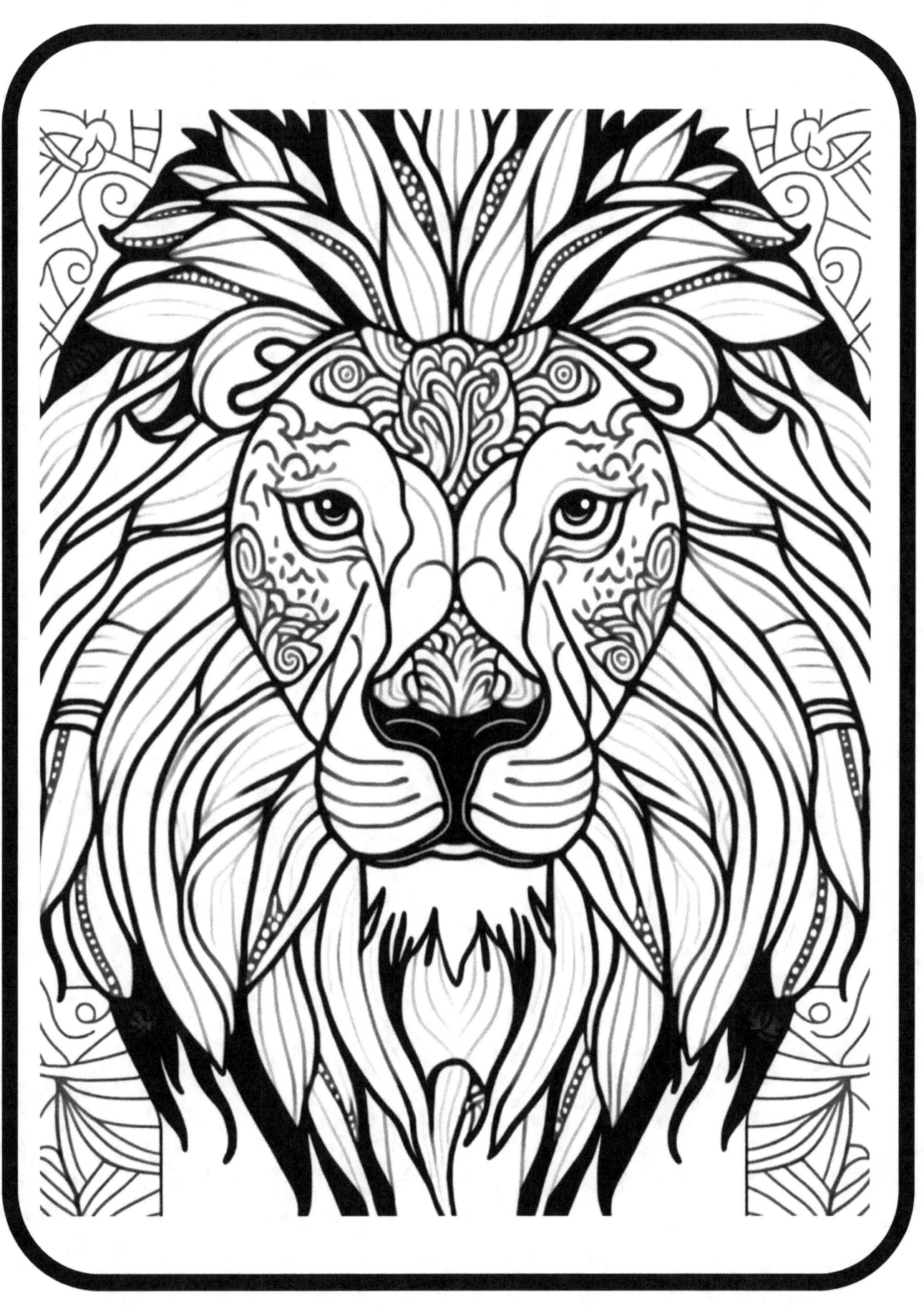

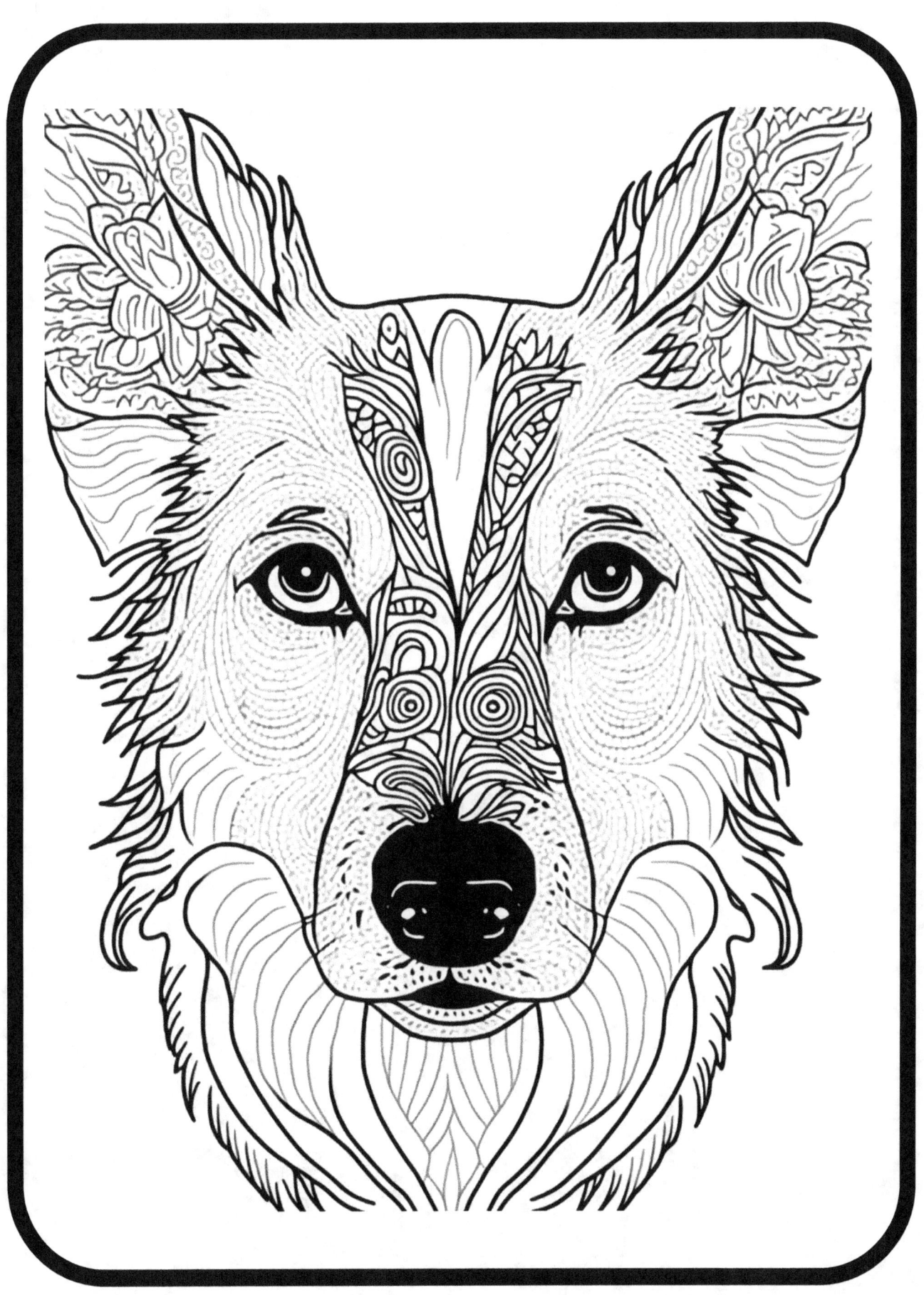

Believe in your creativity.

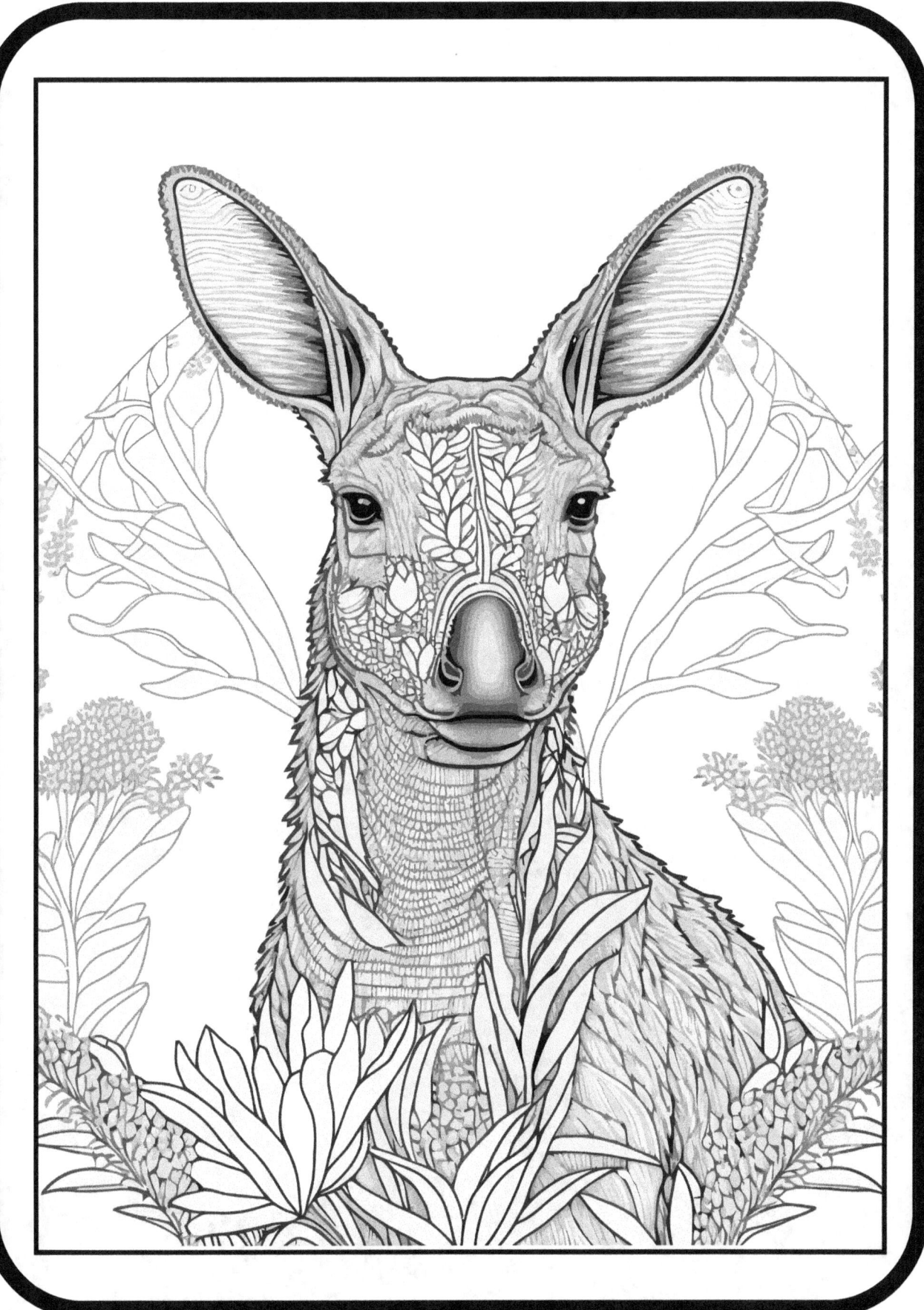

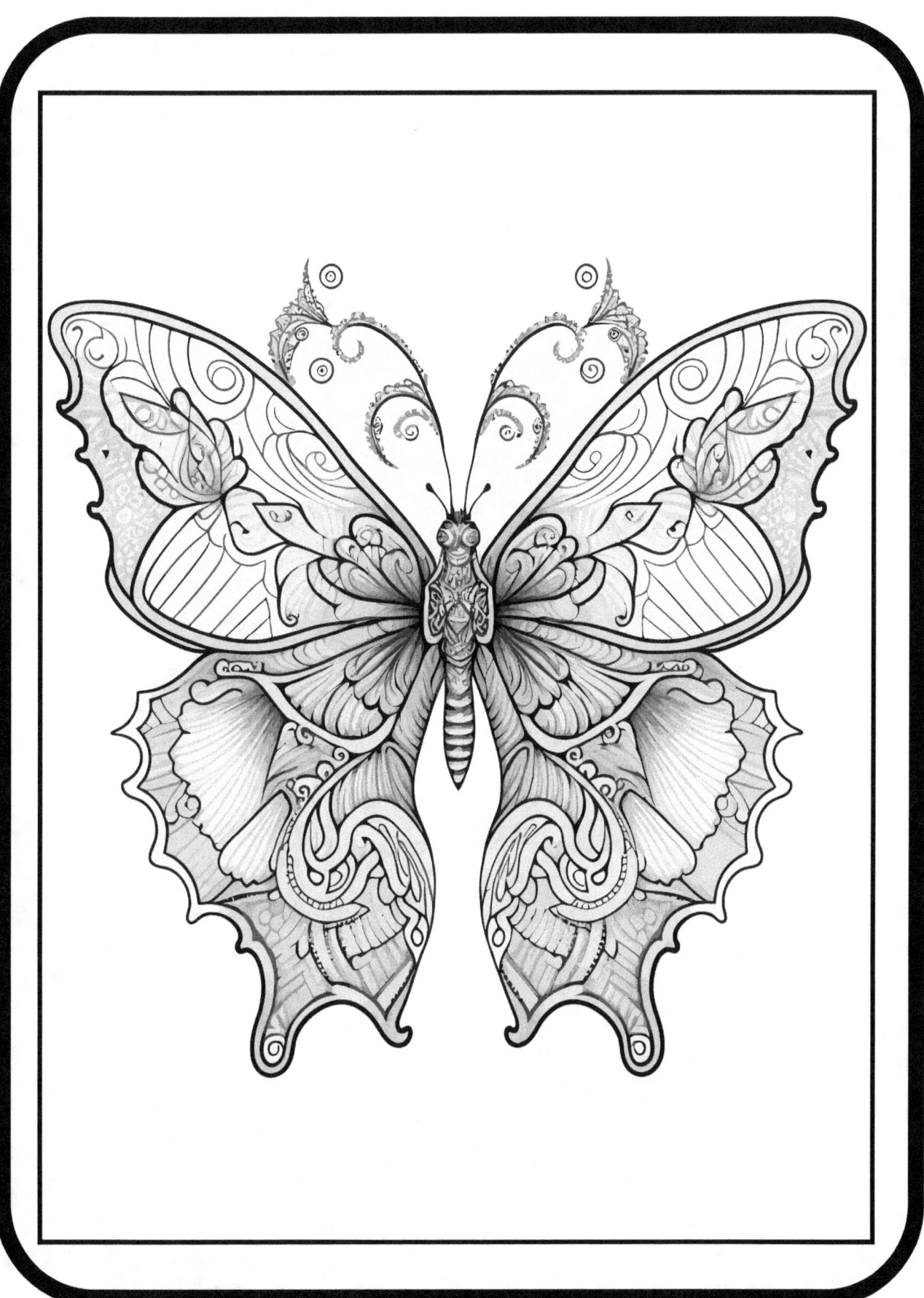

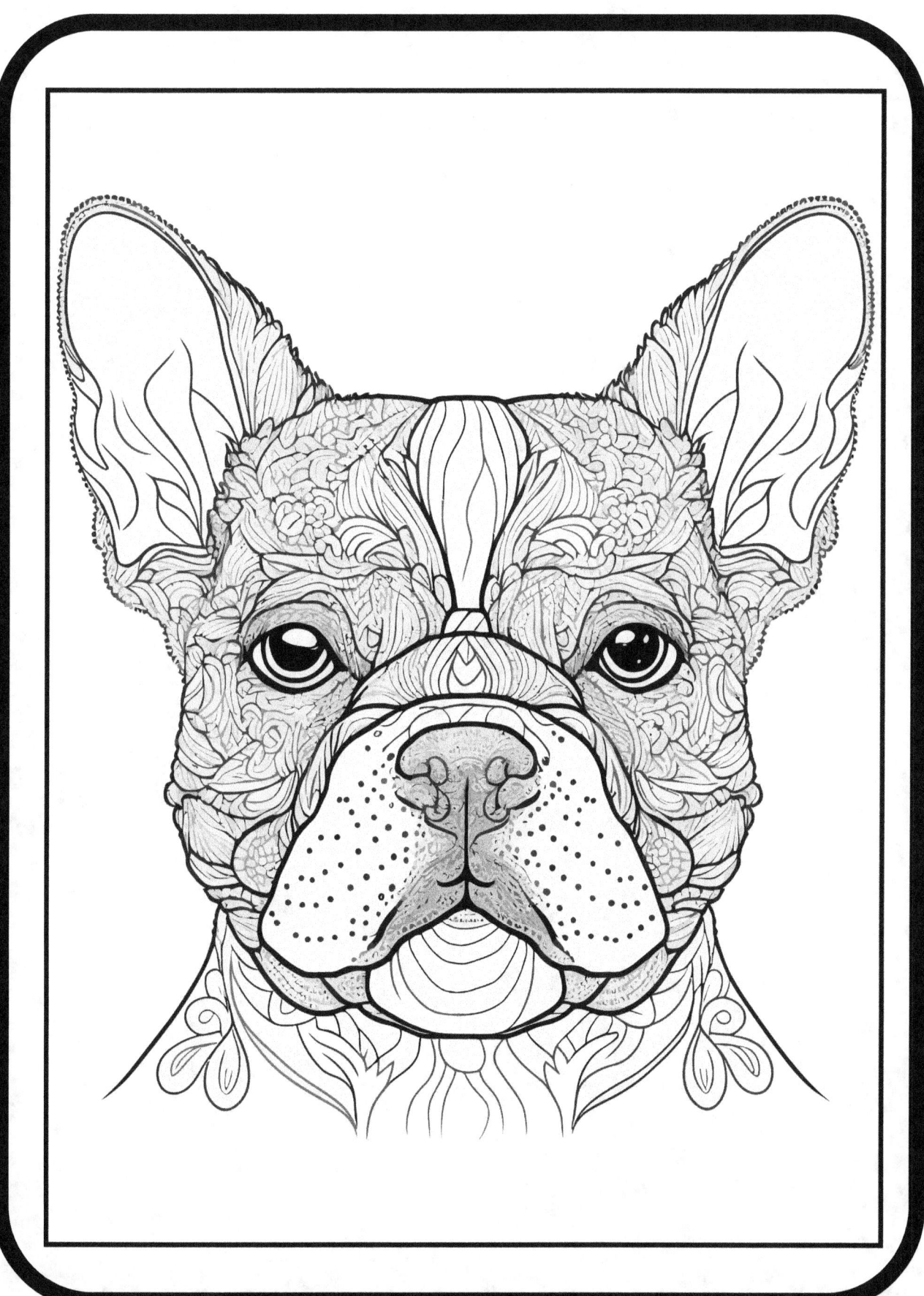

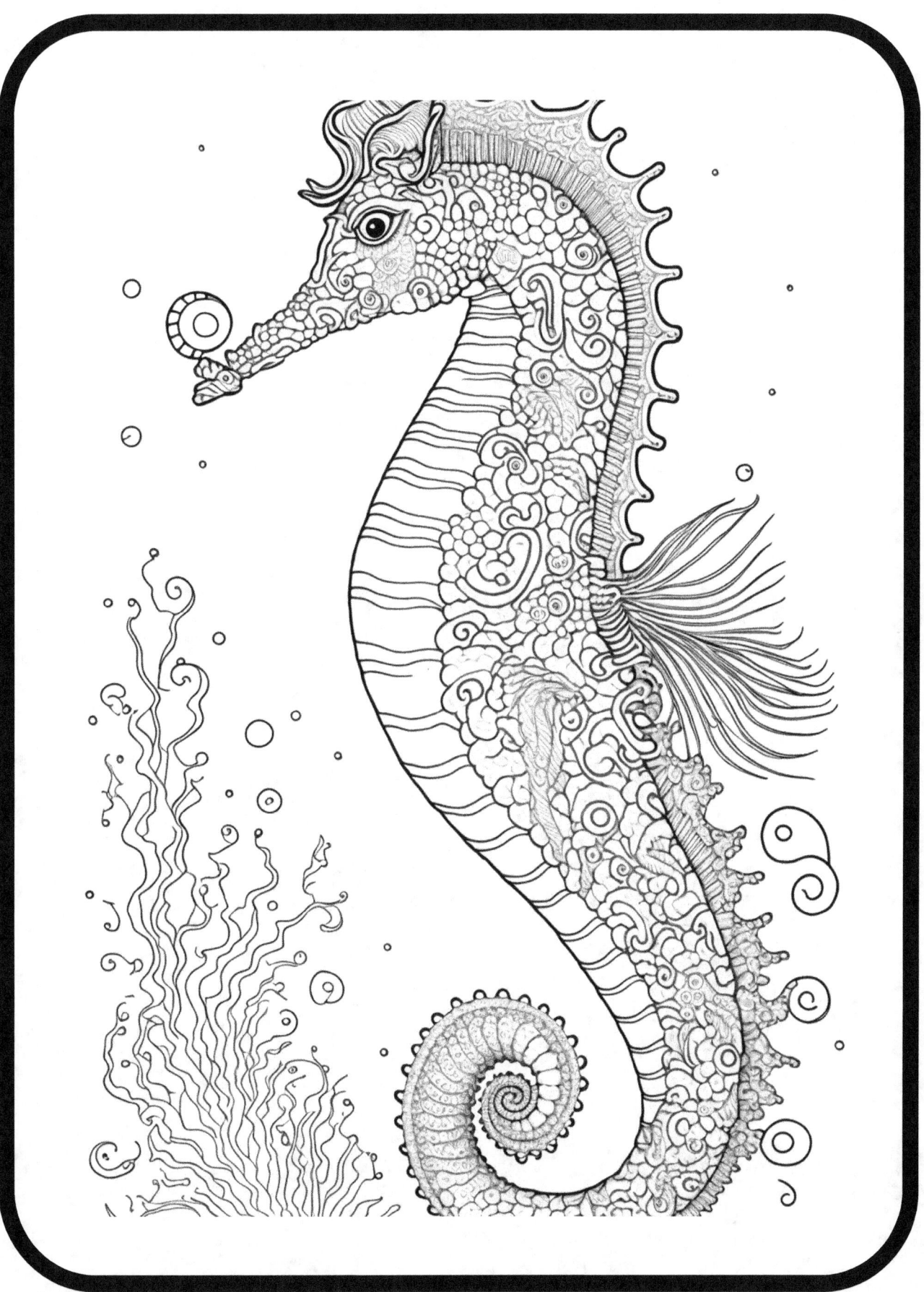

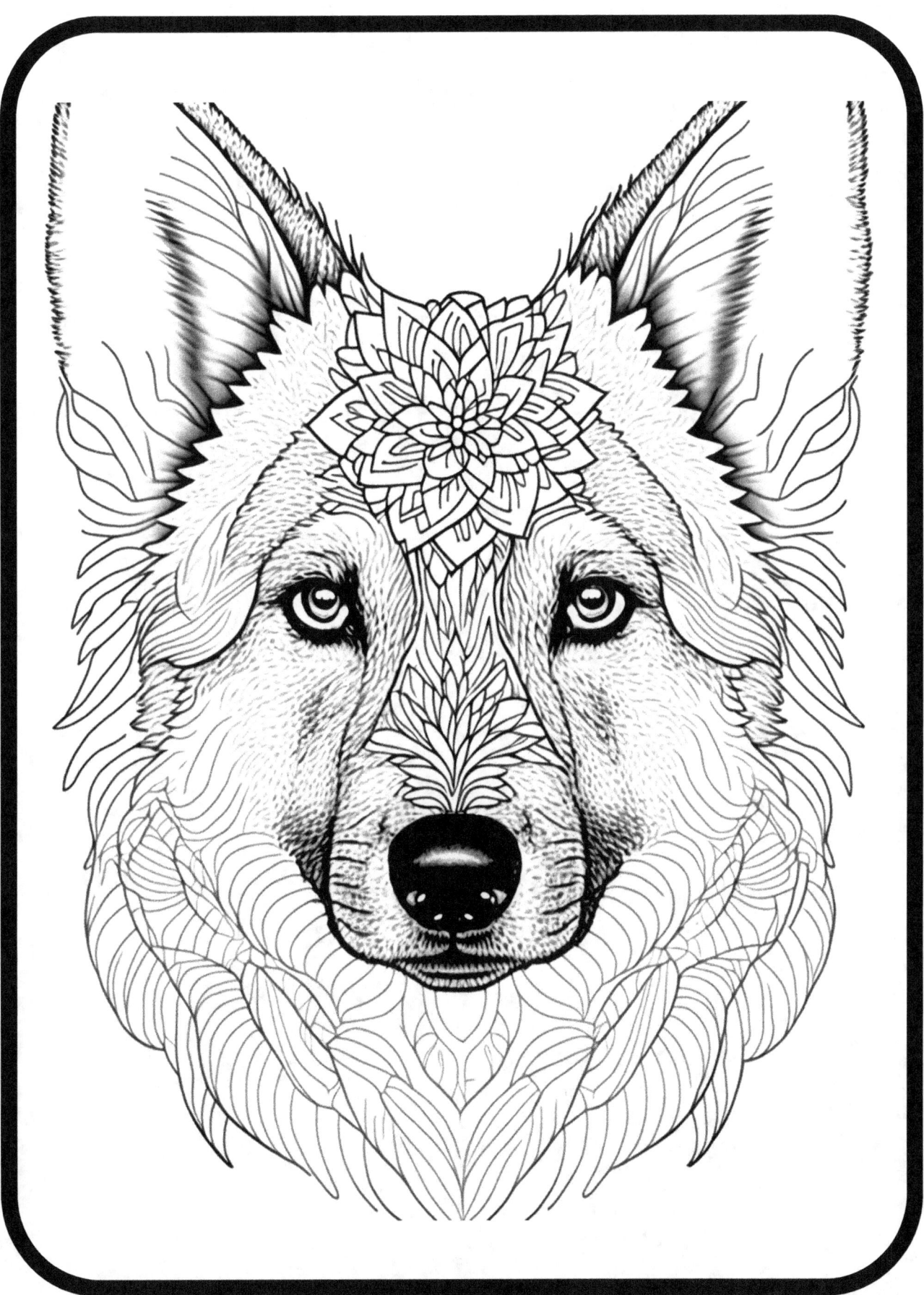

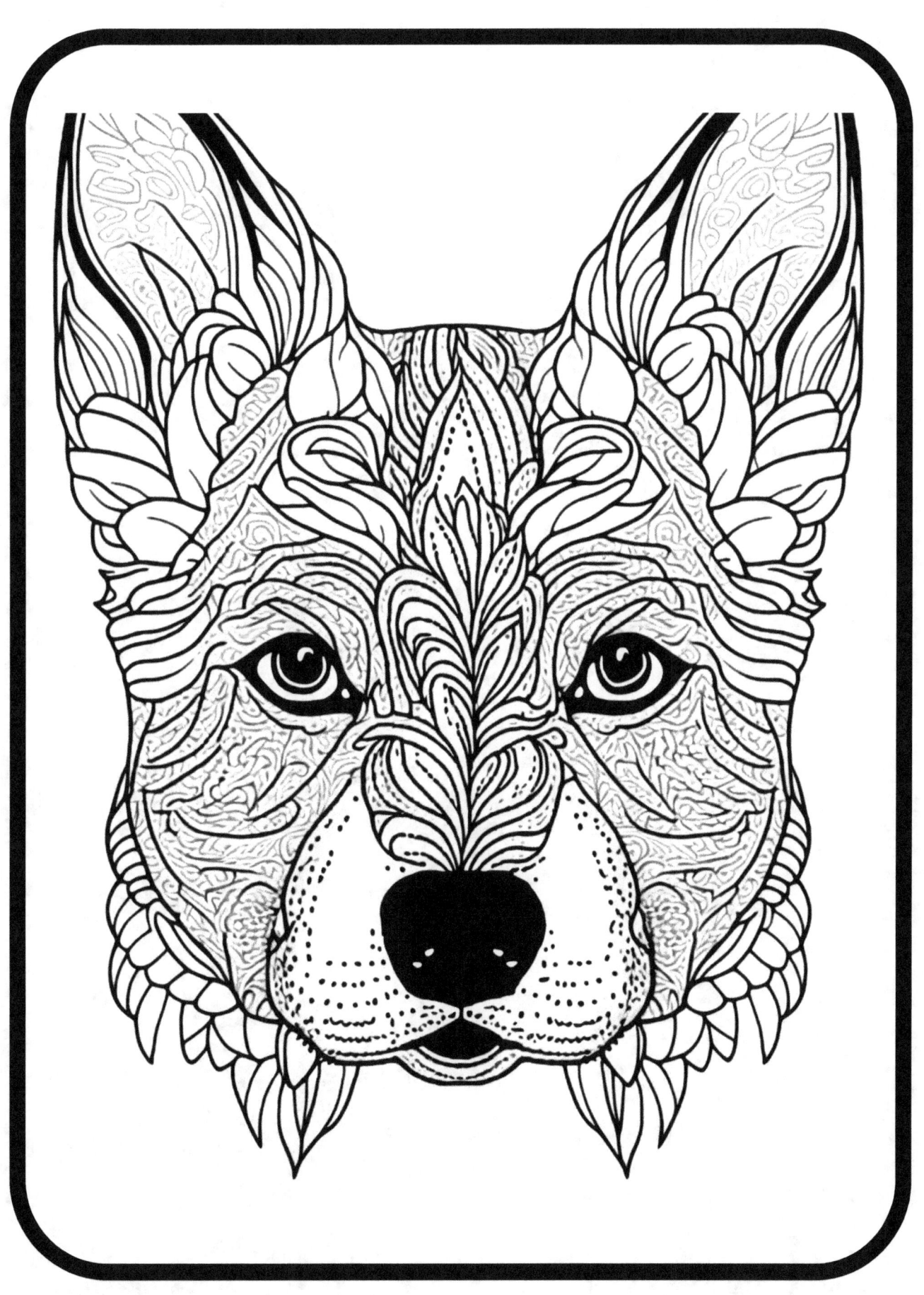

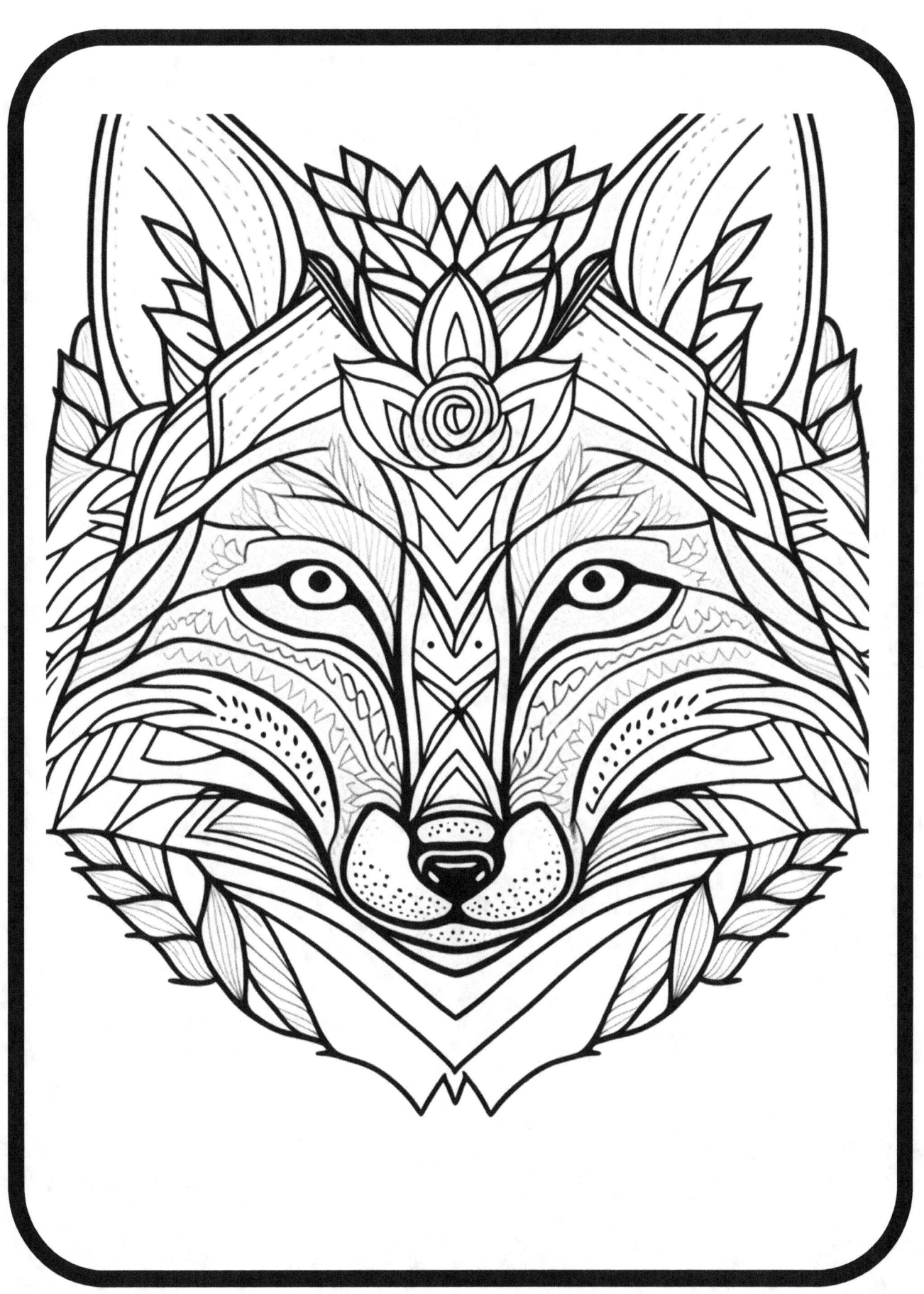

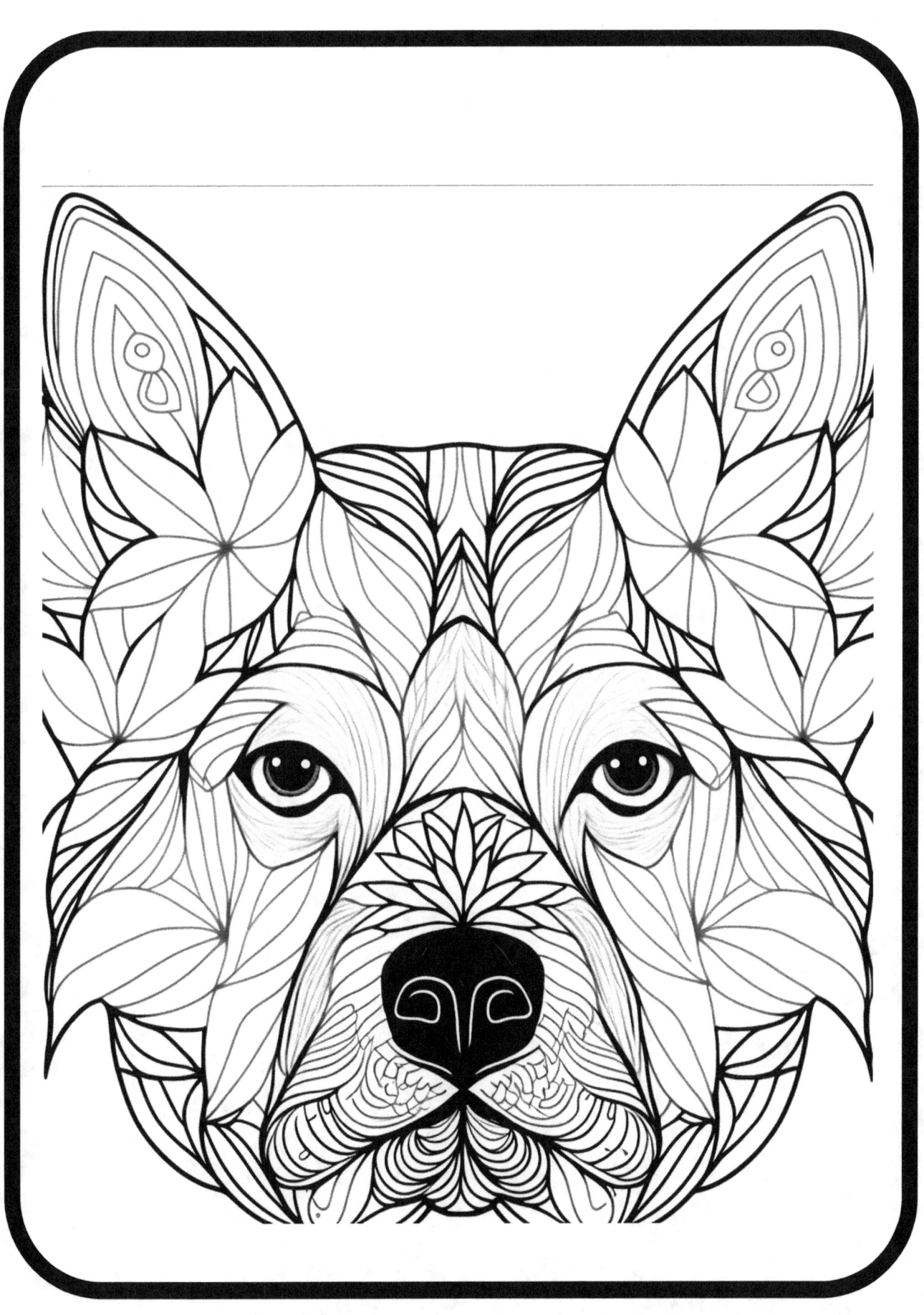

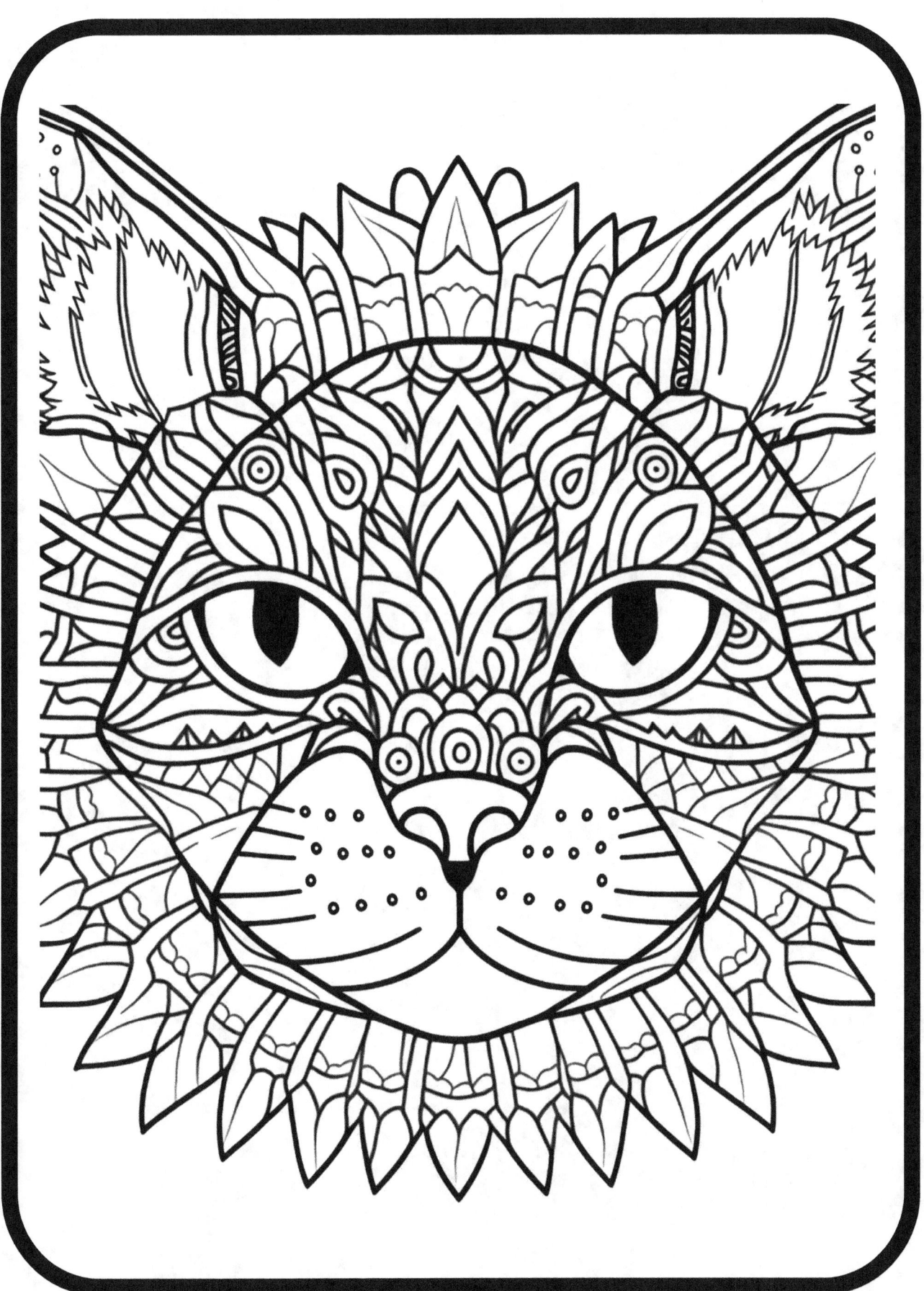

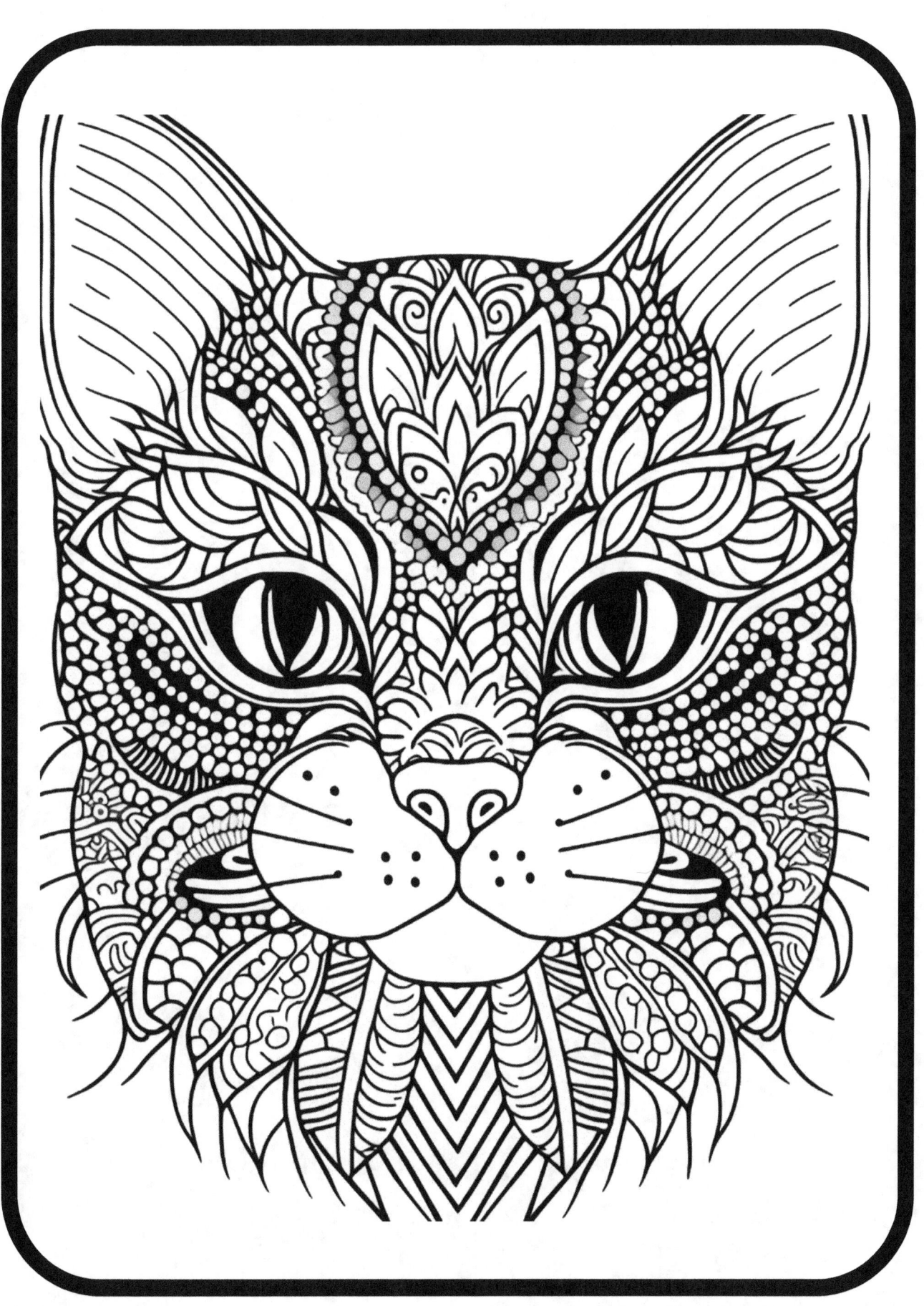

Keep fighting for your dreams.

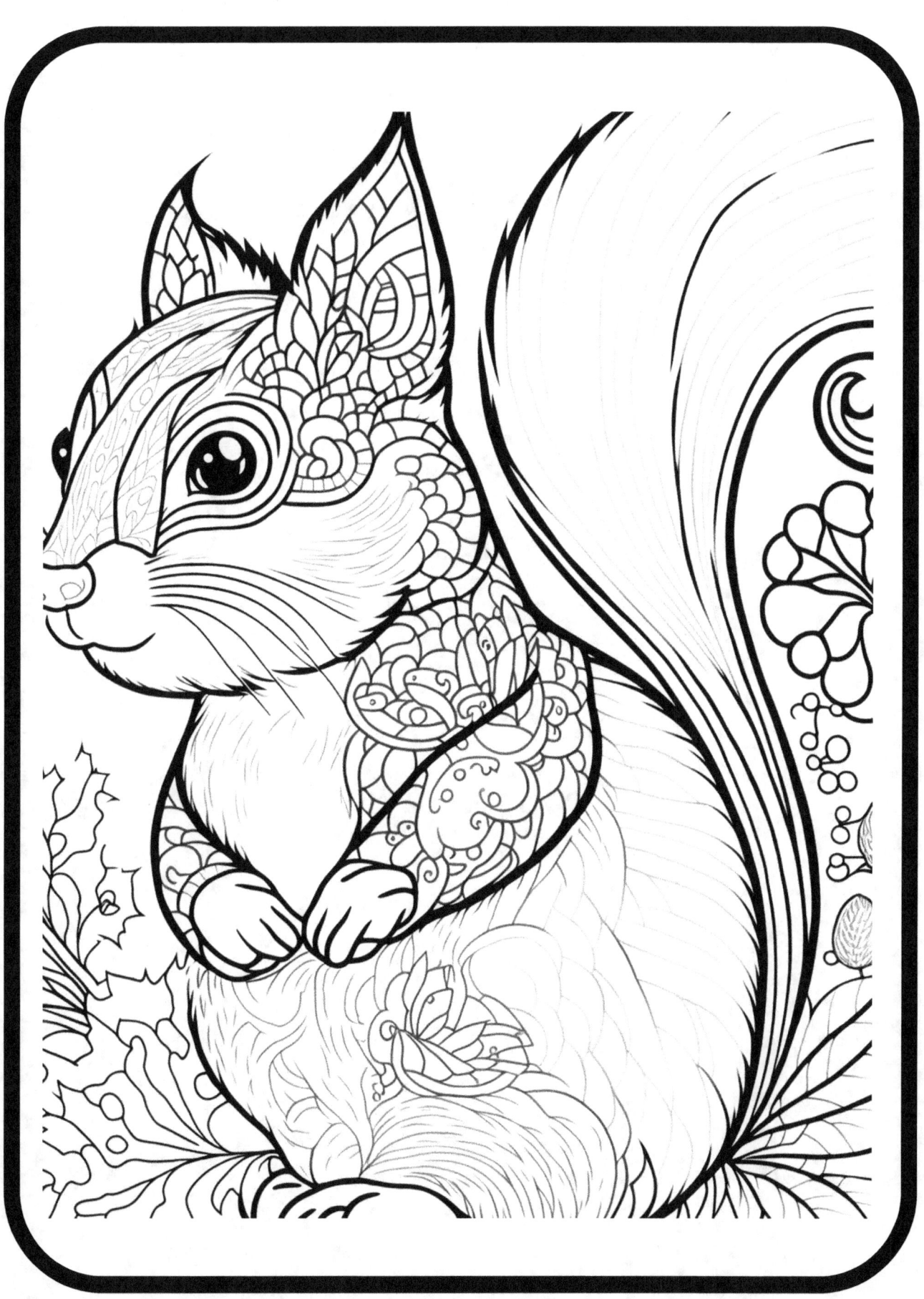

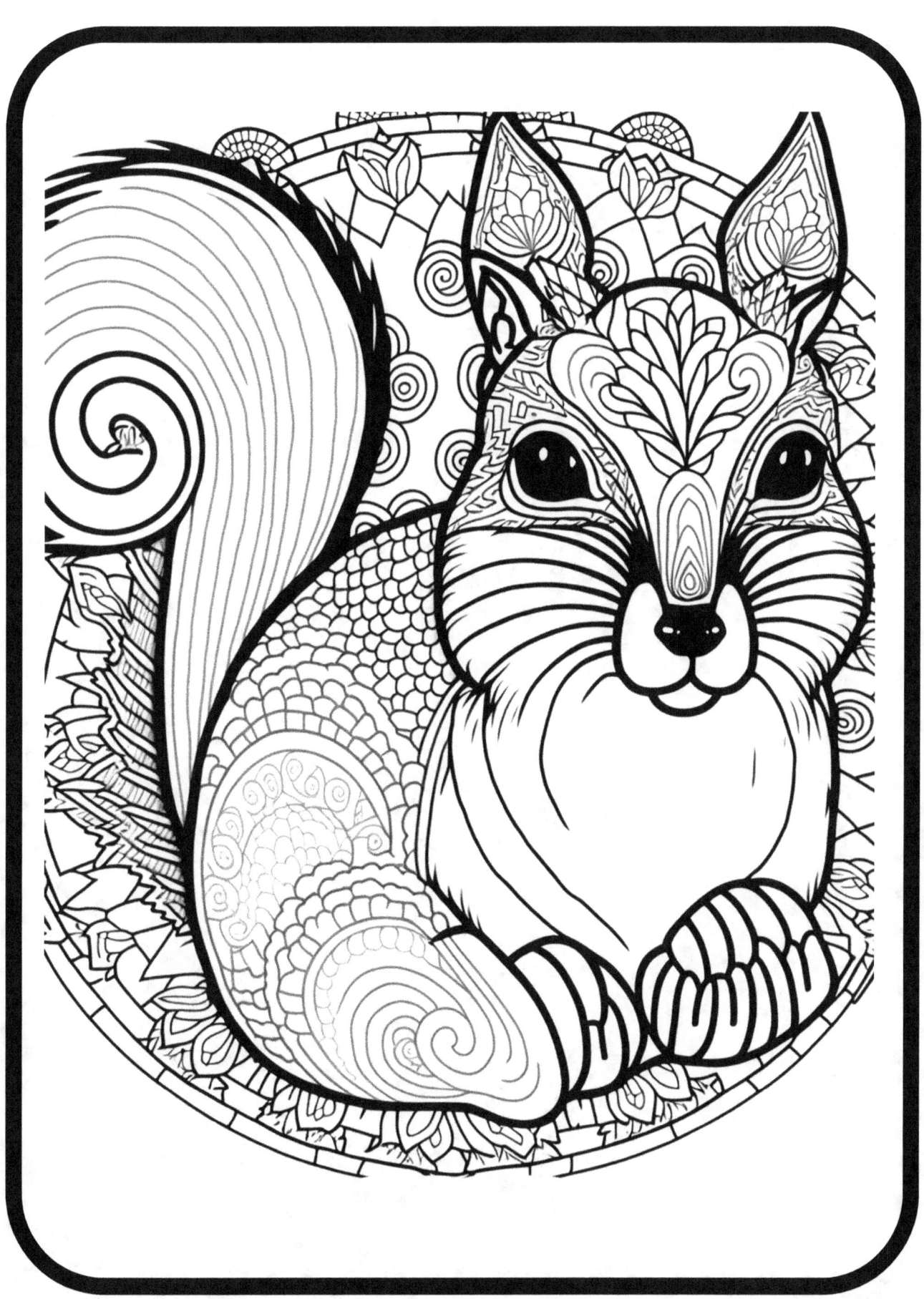

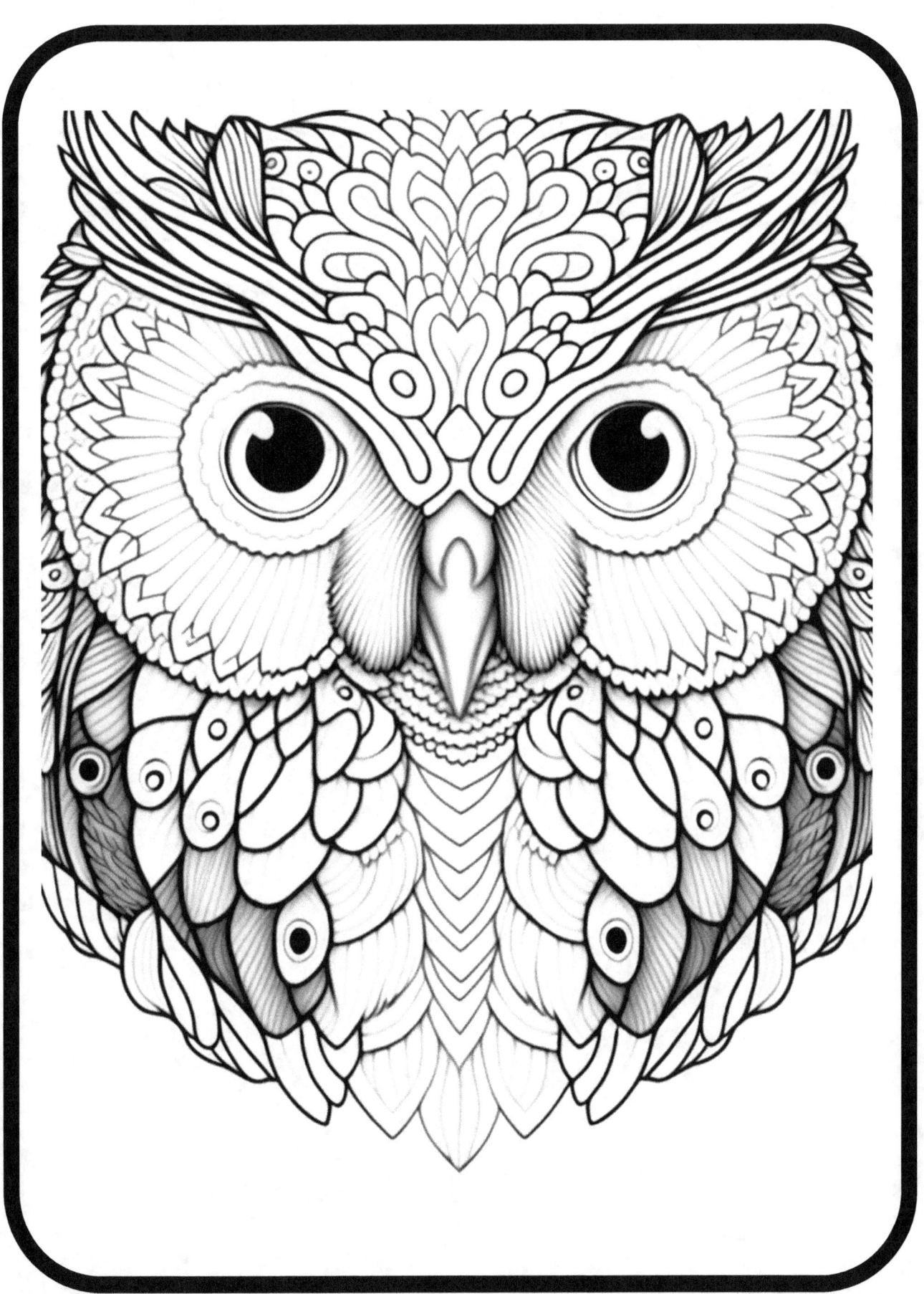

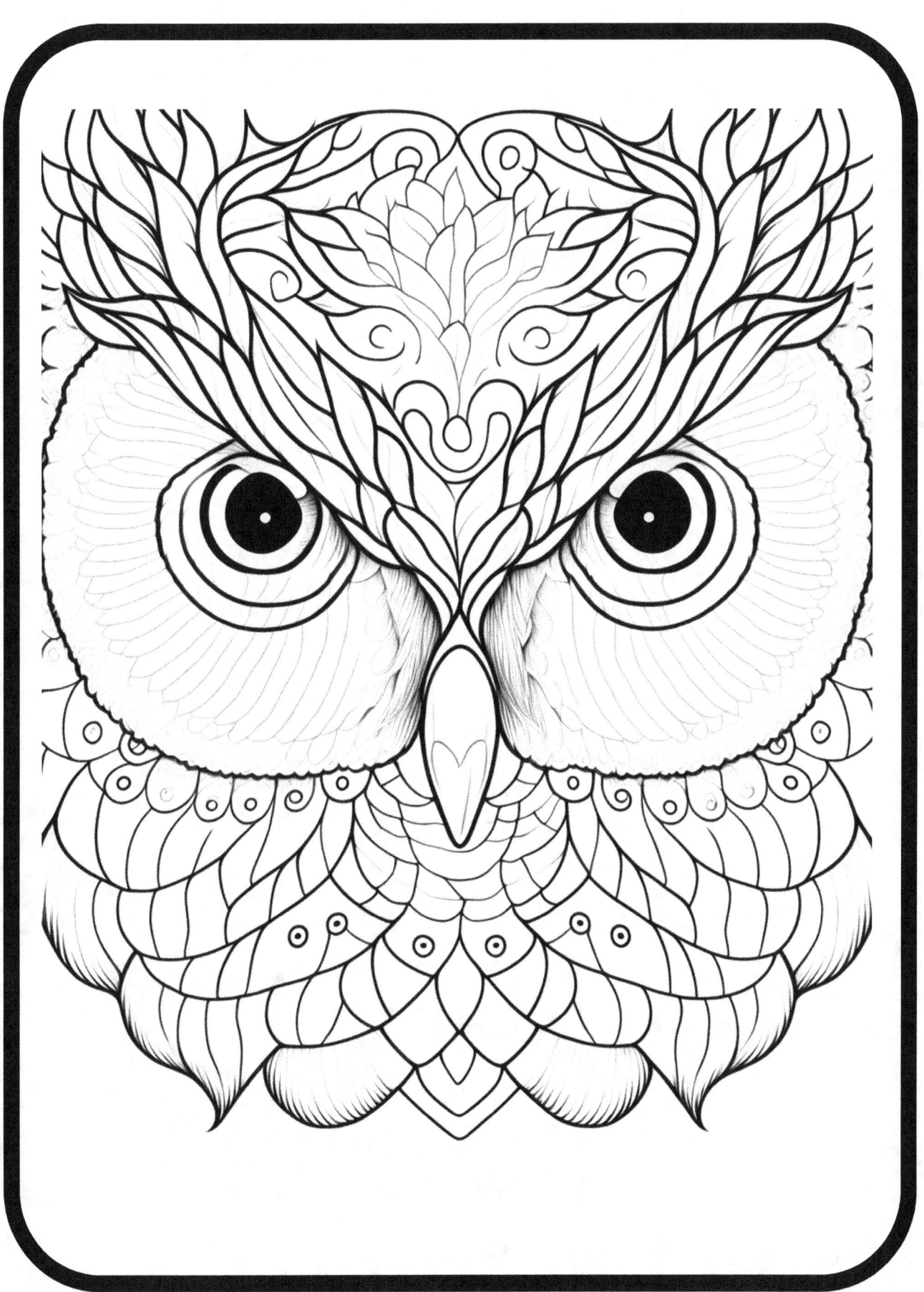

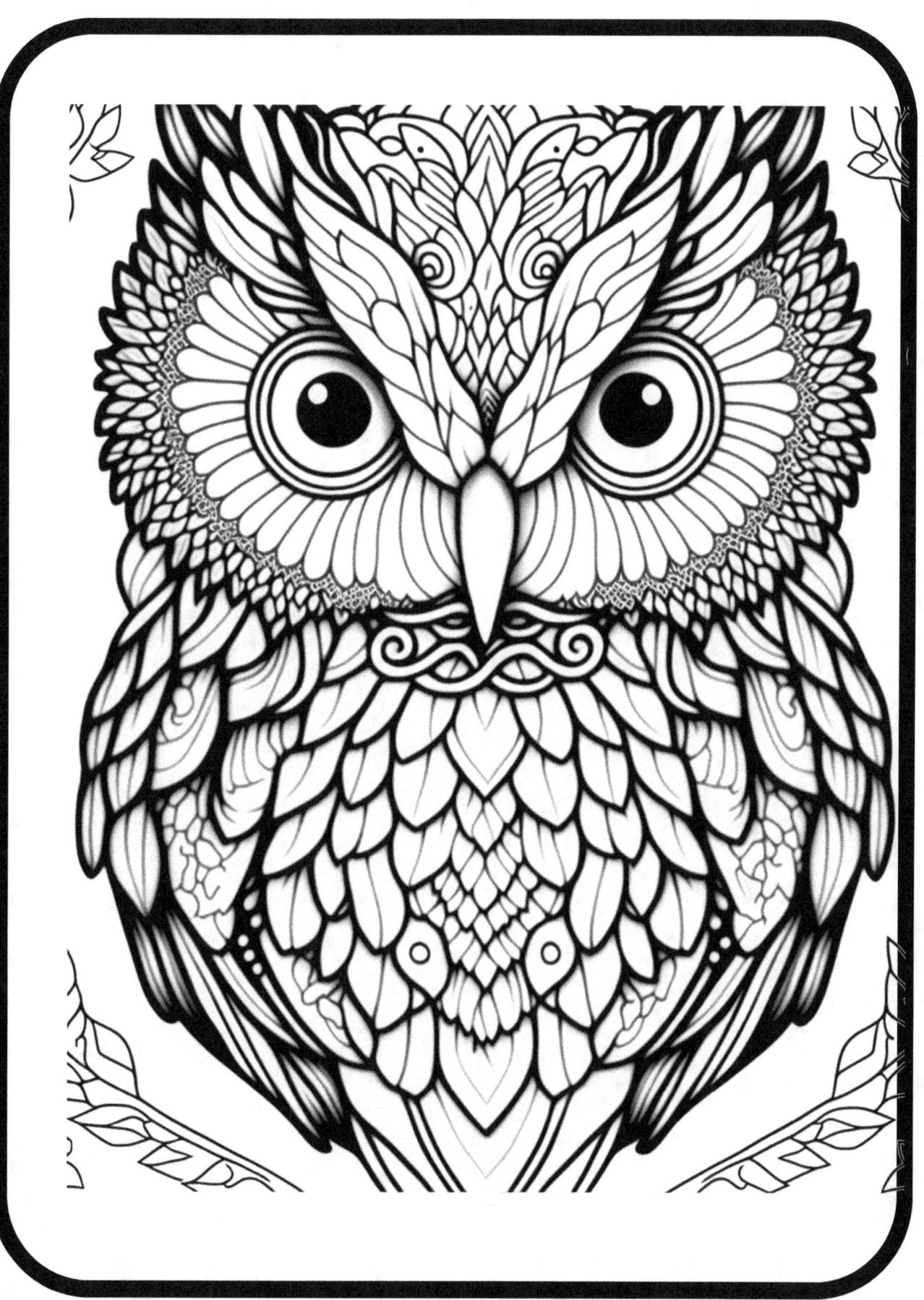

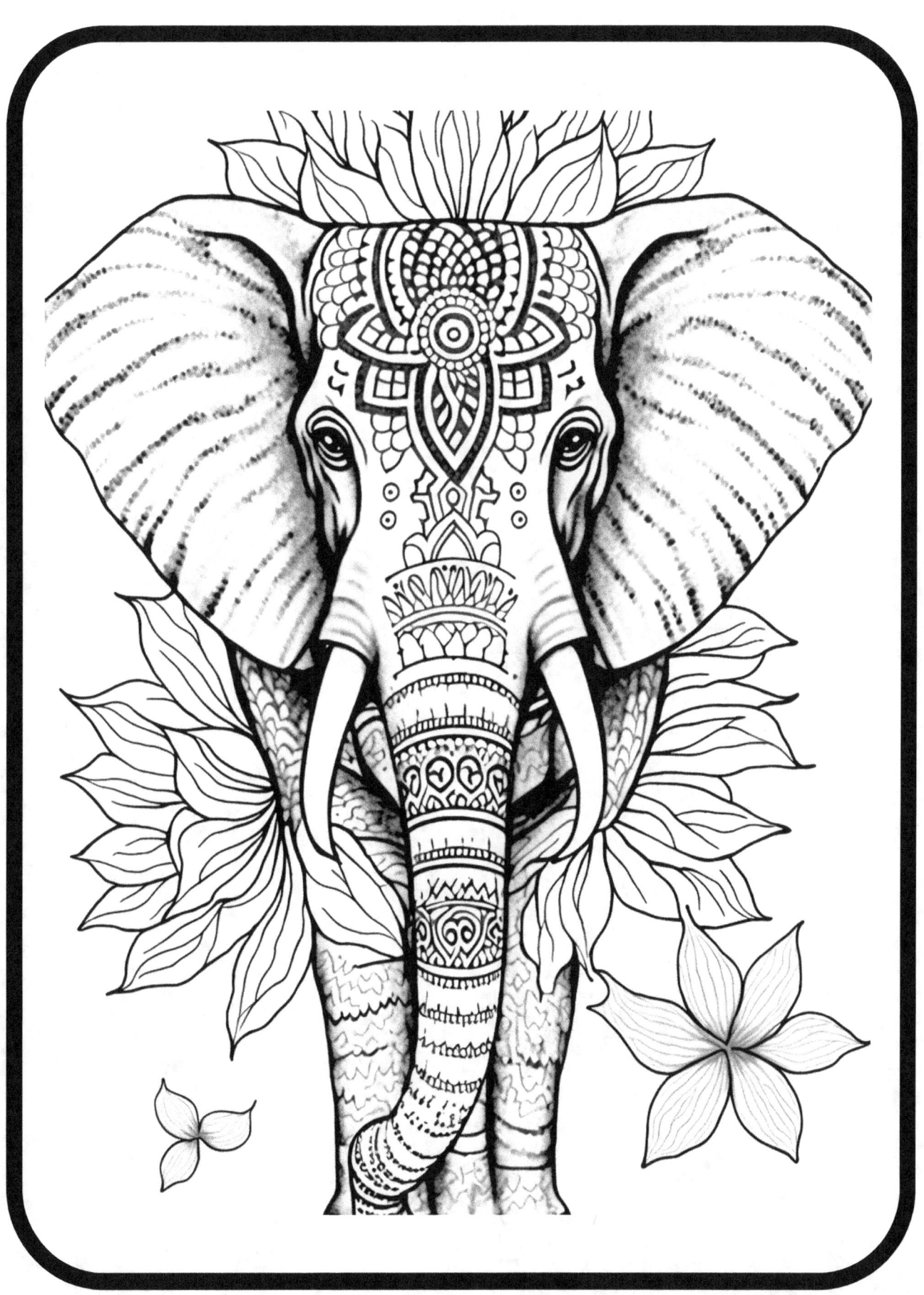

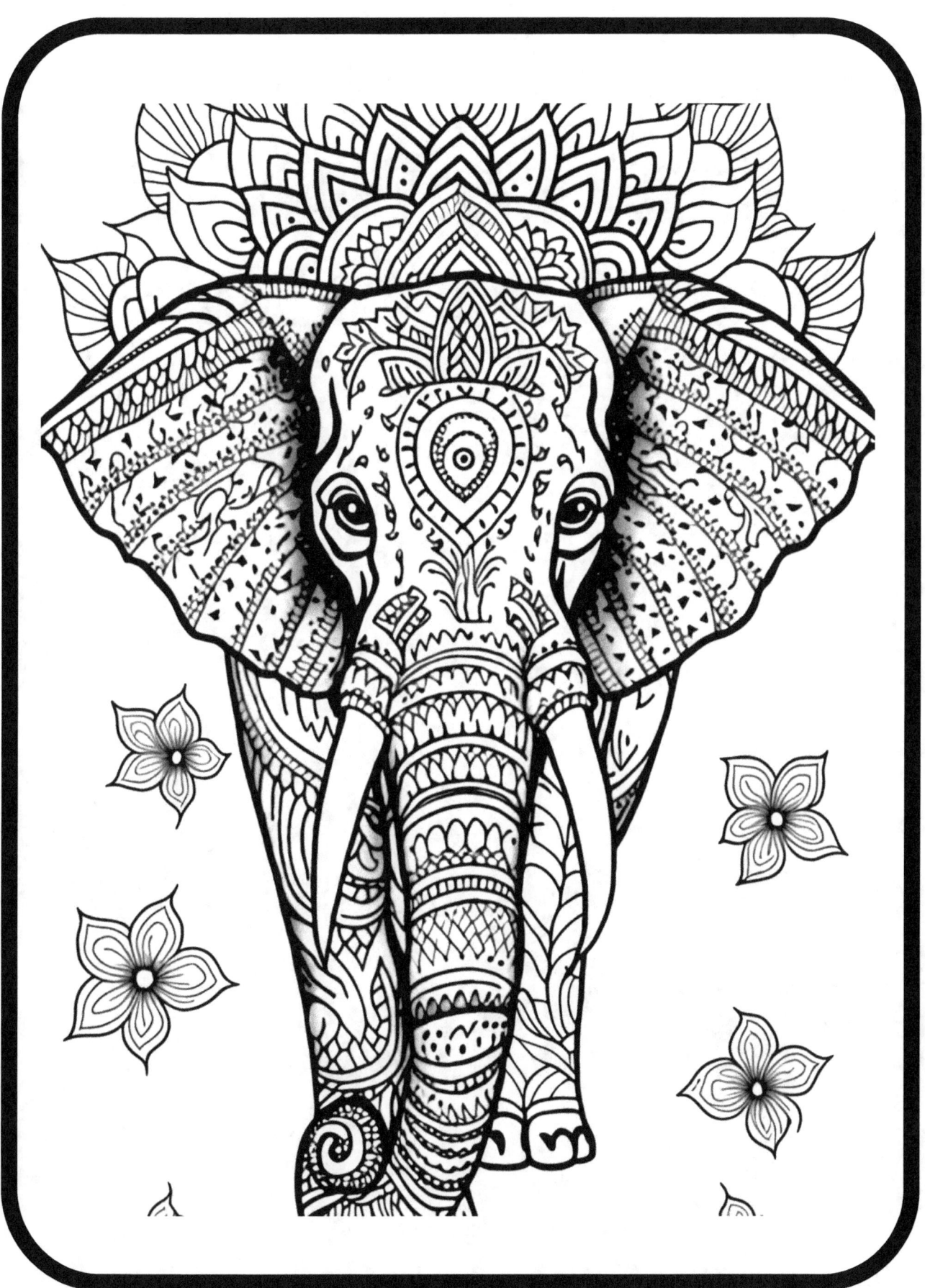

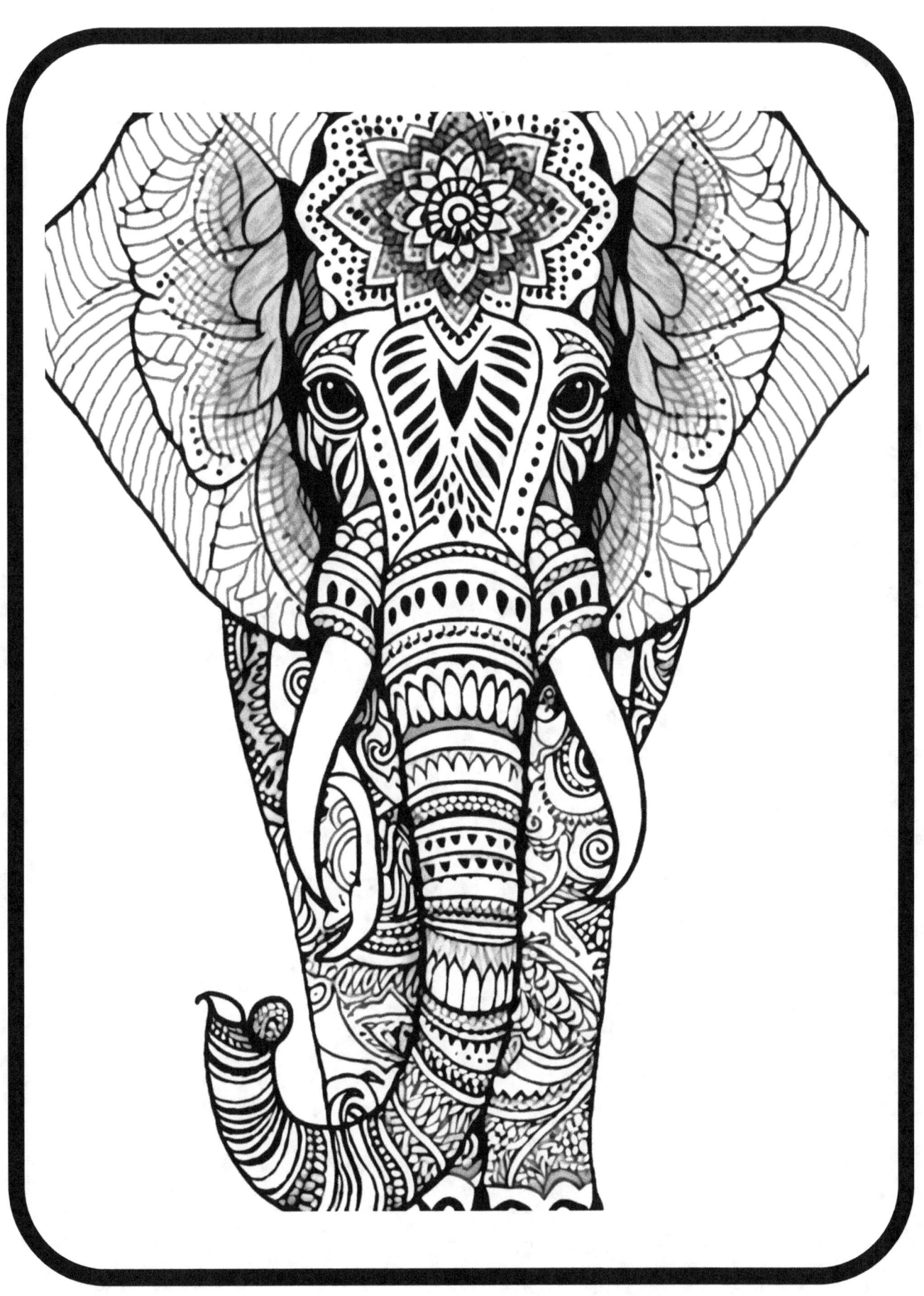

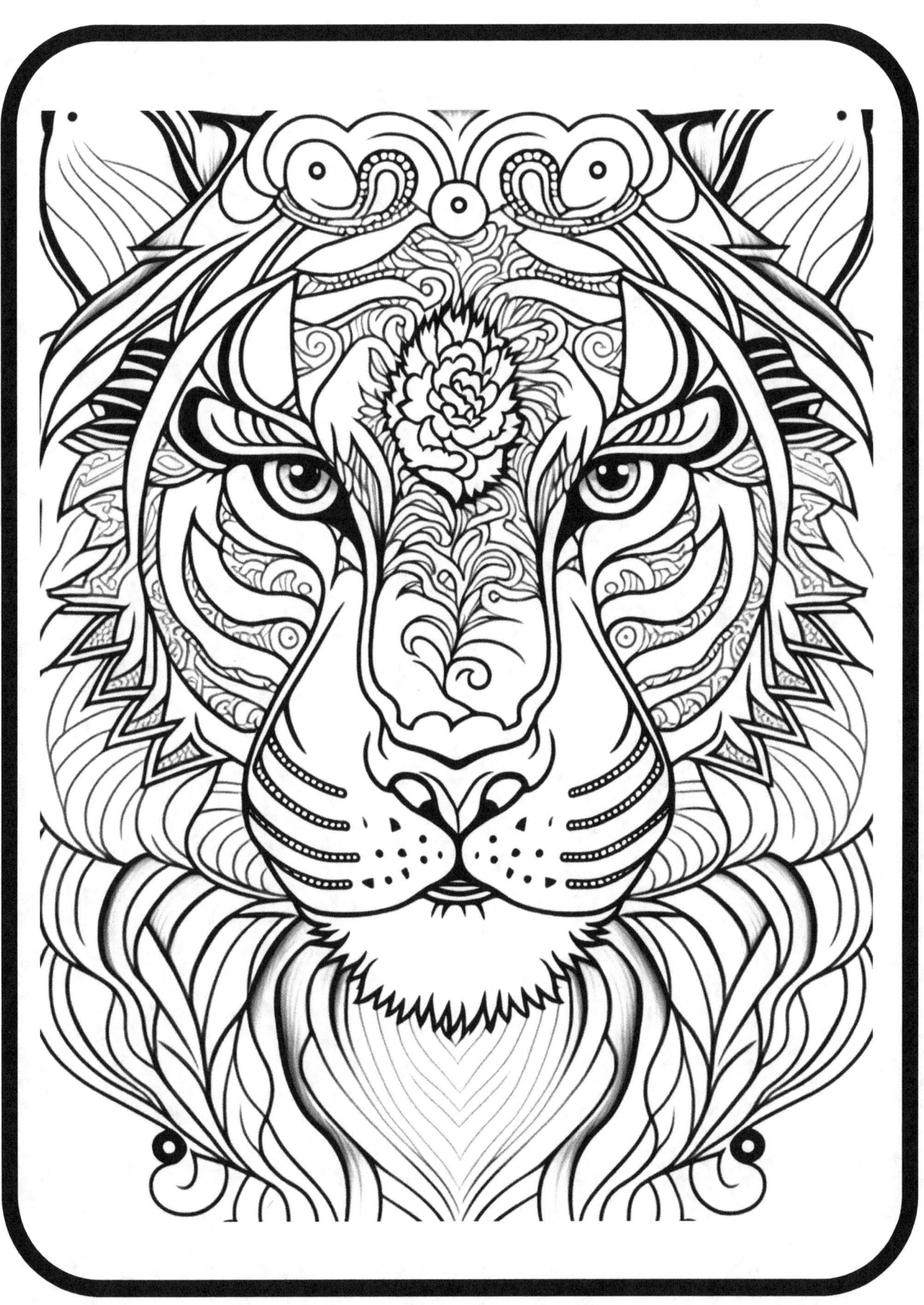

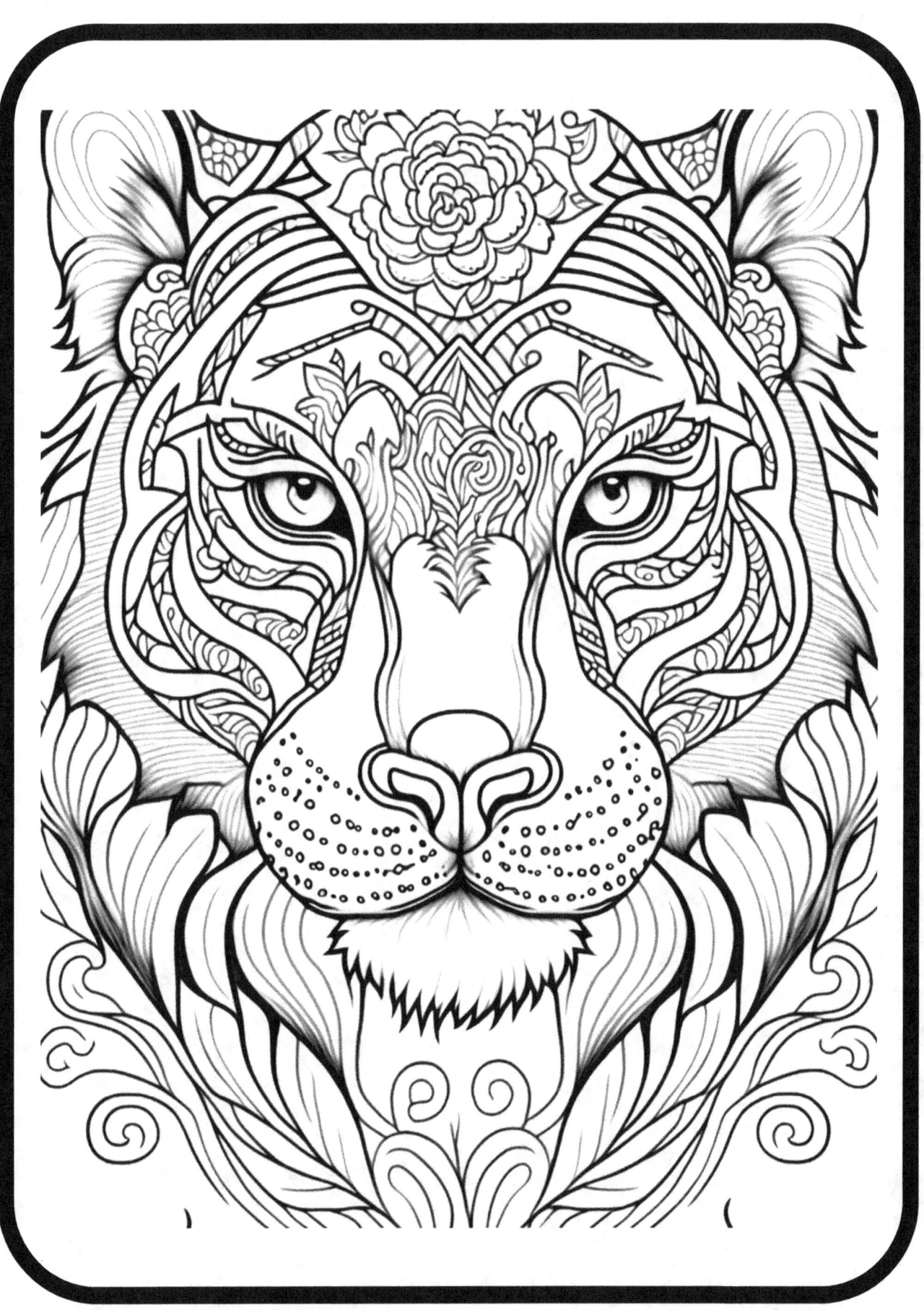

You have the power within.

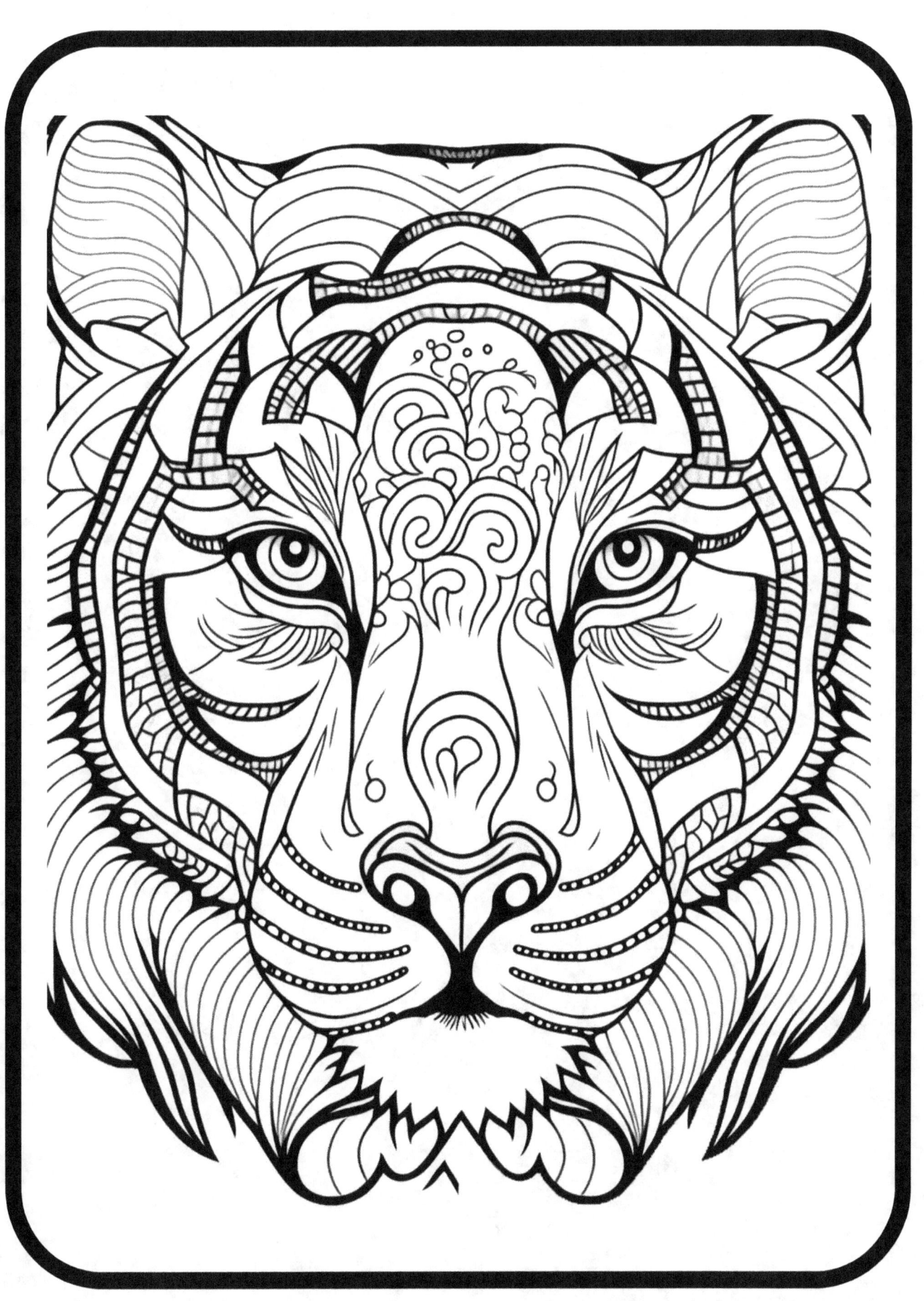

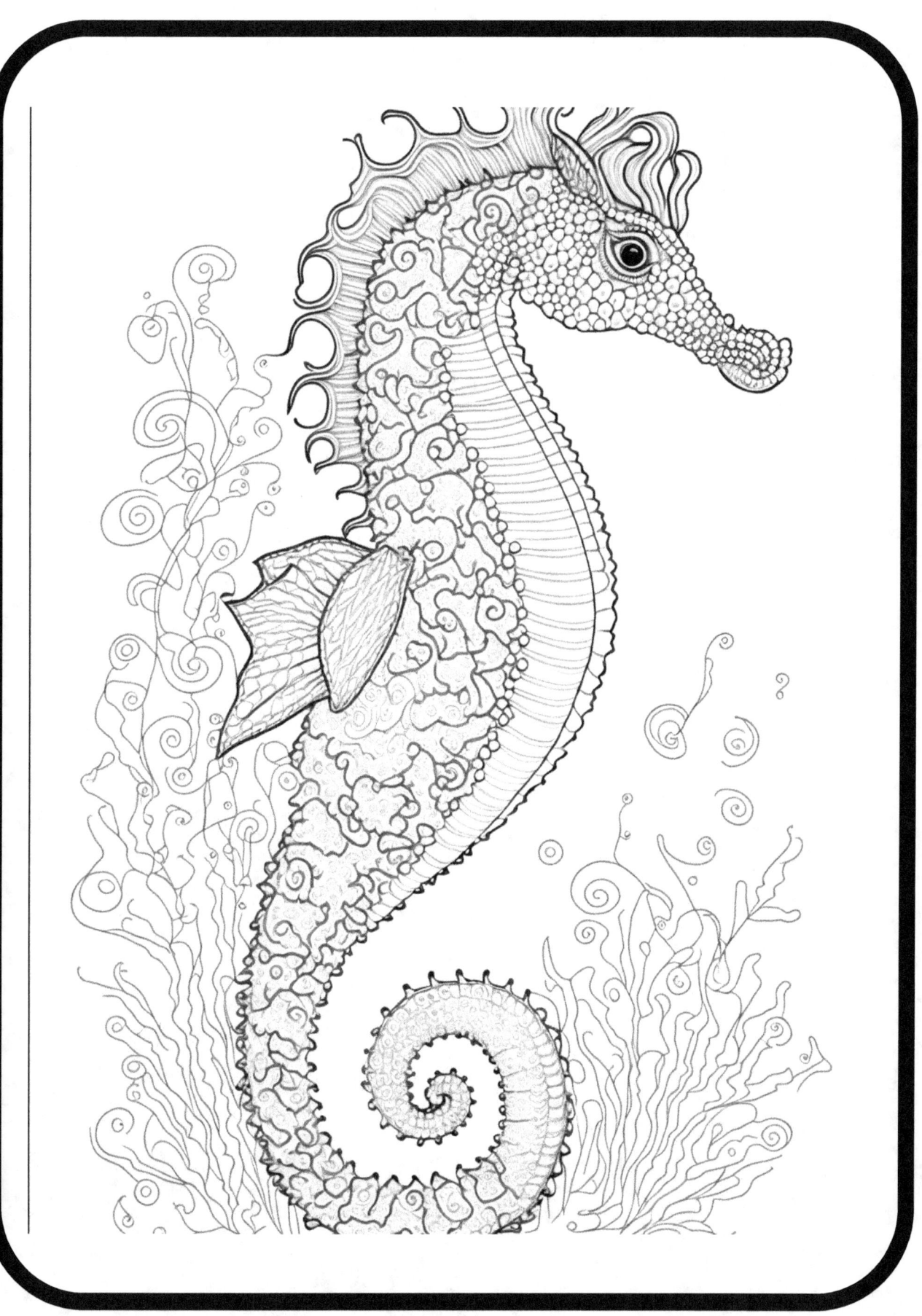

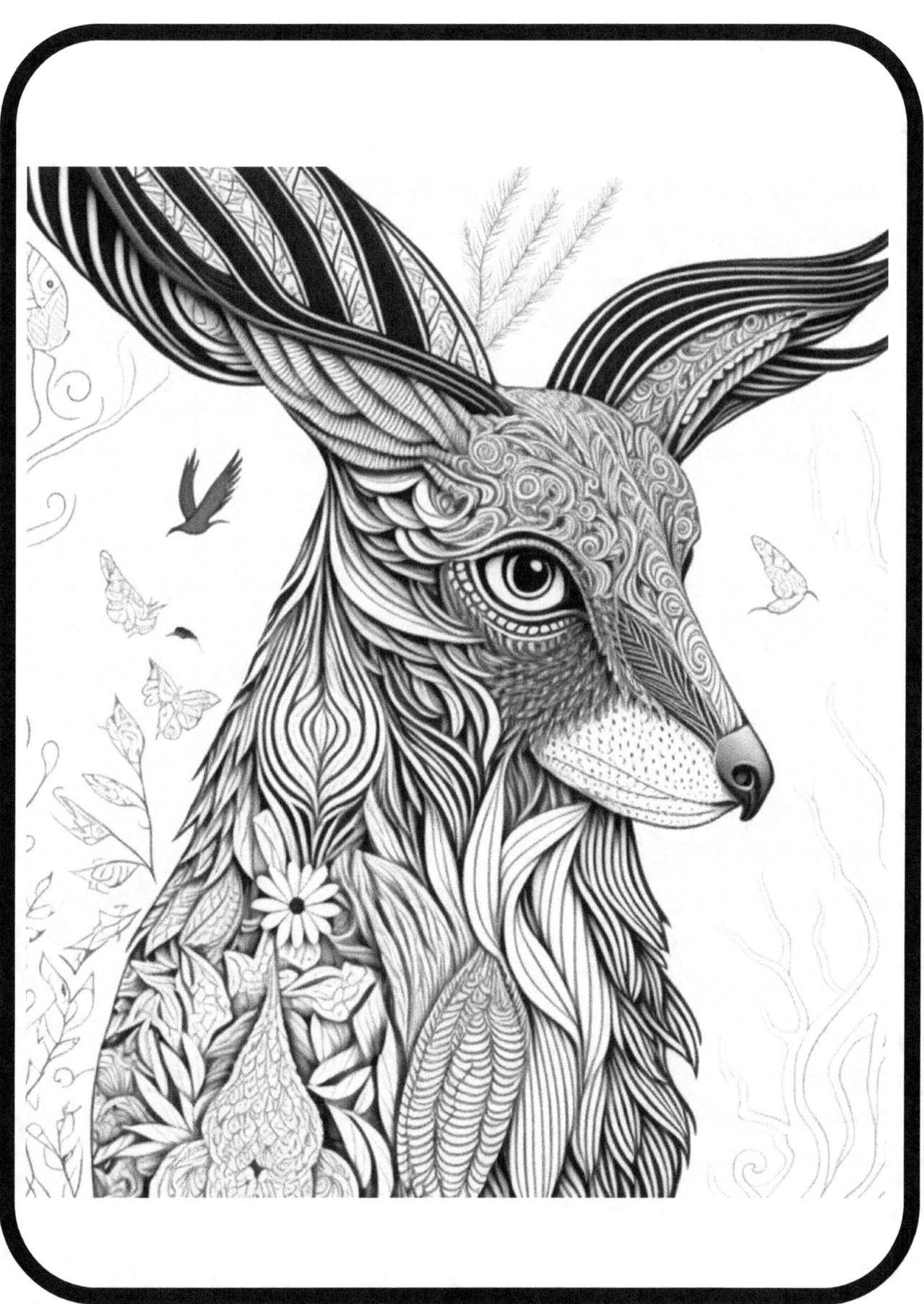

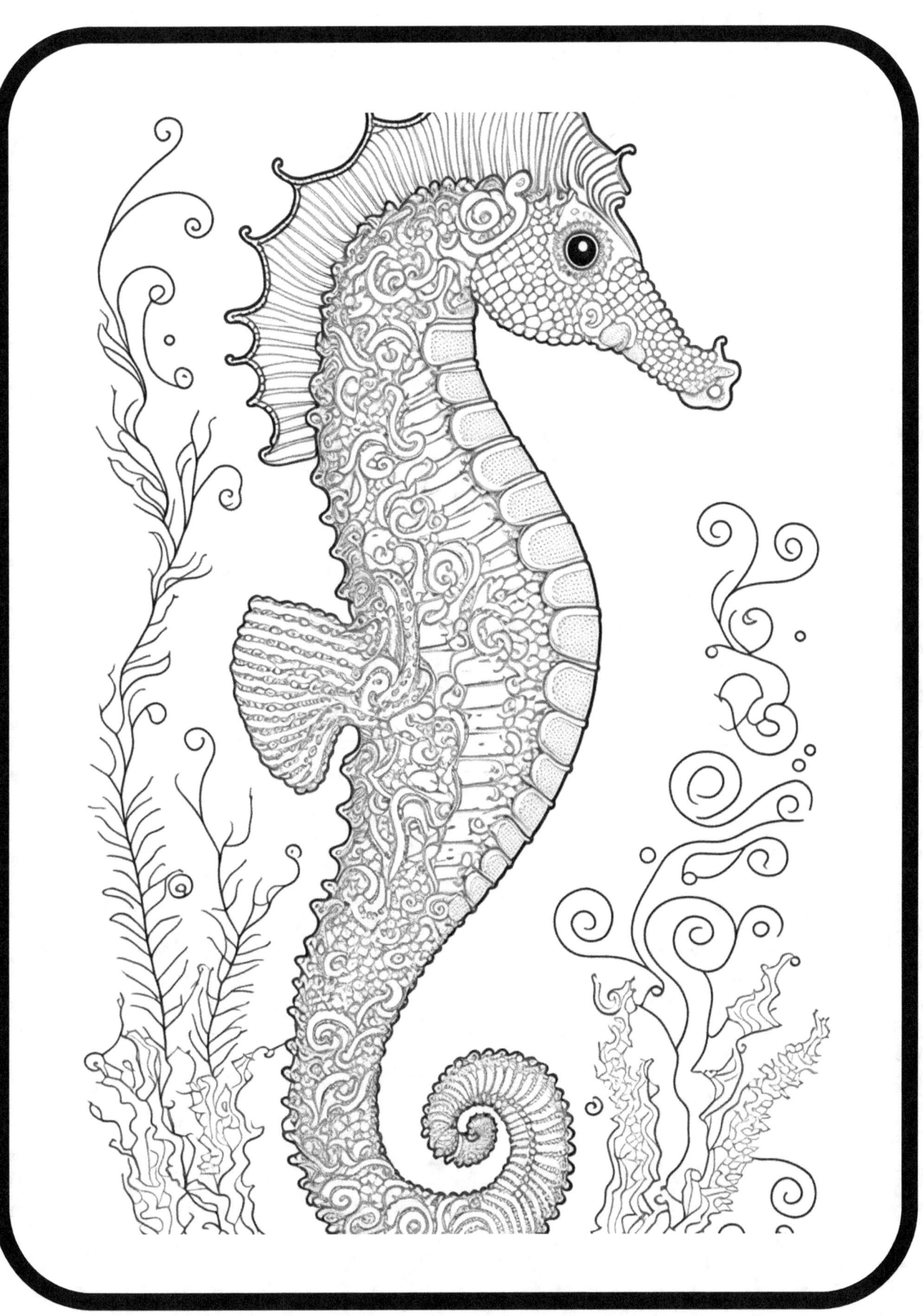

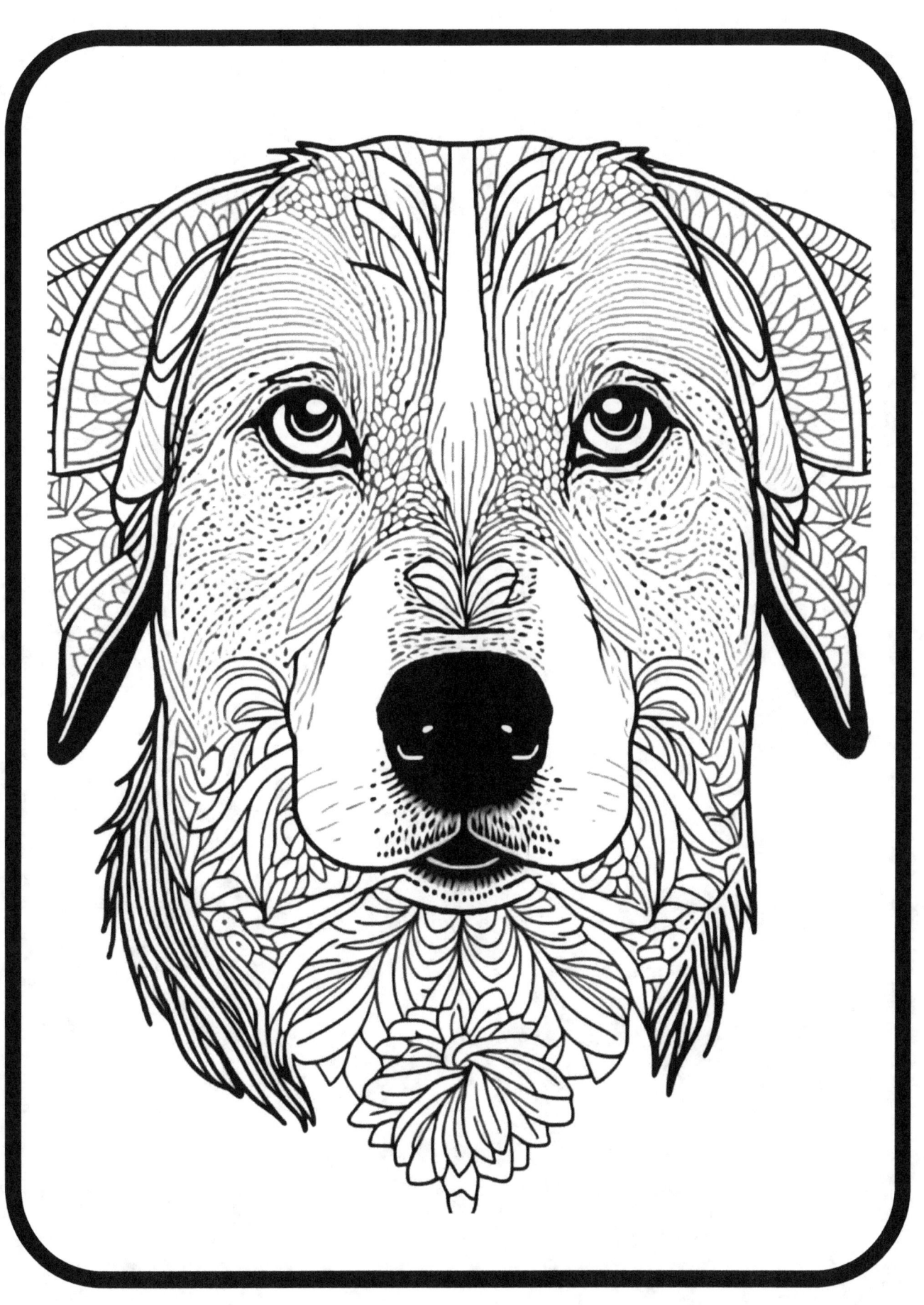

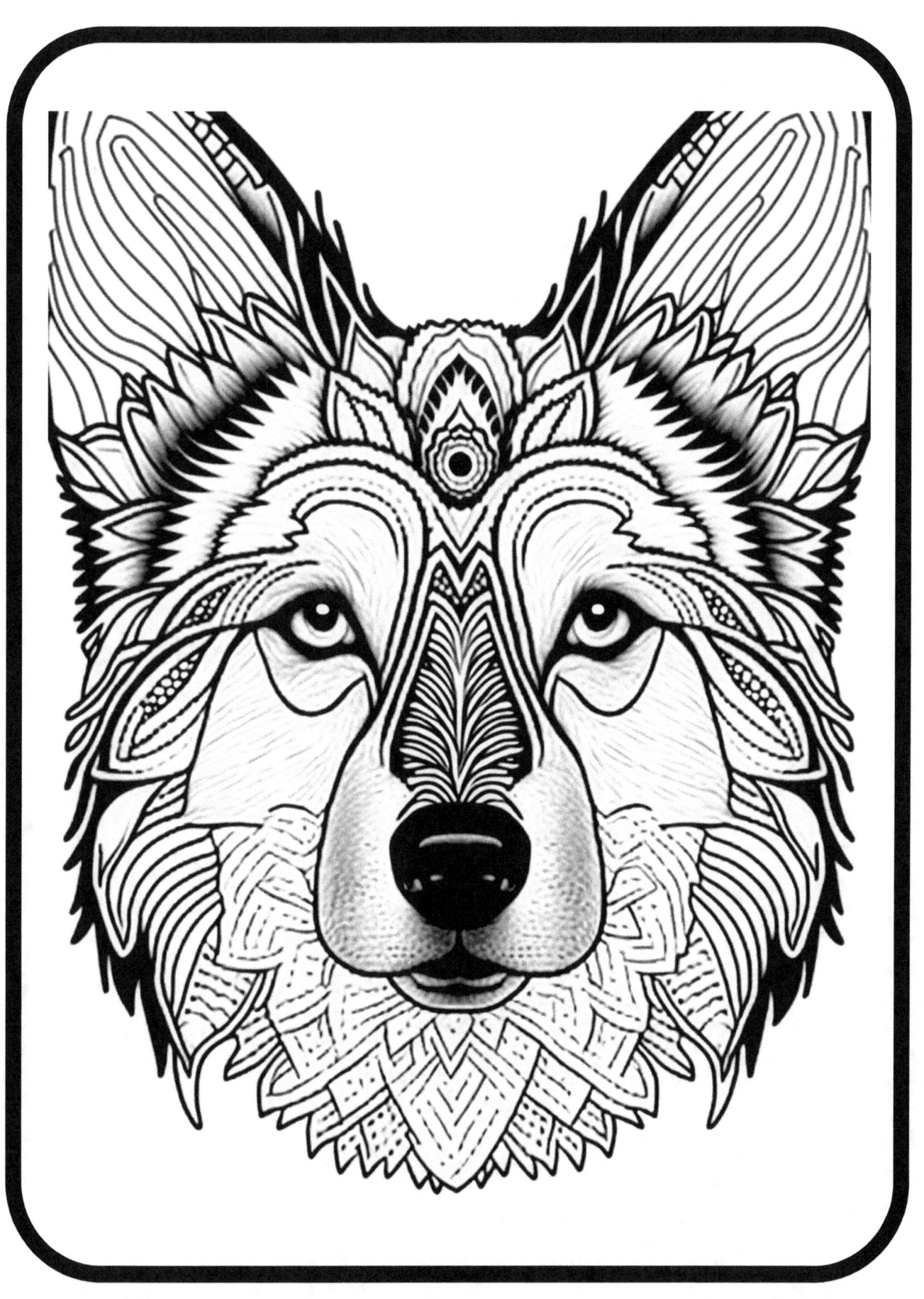

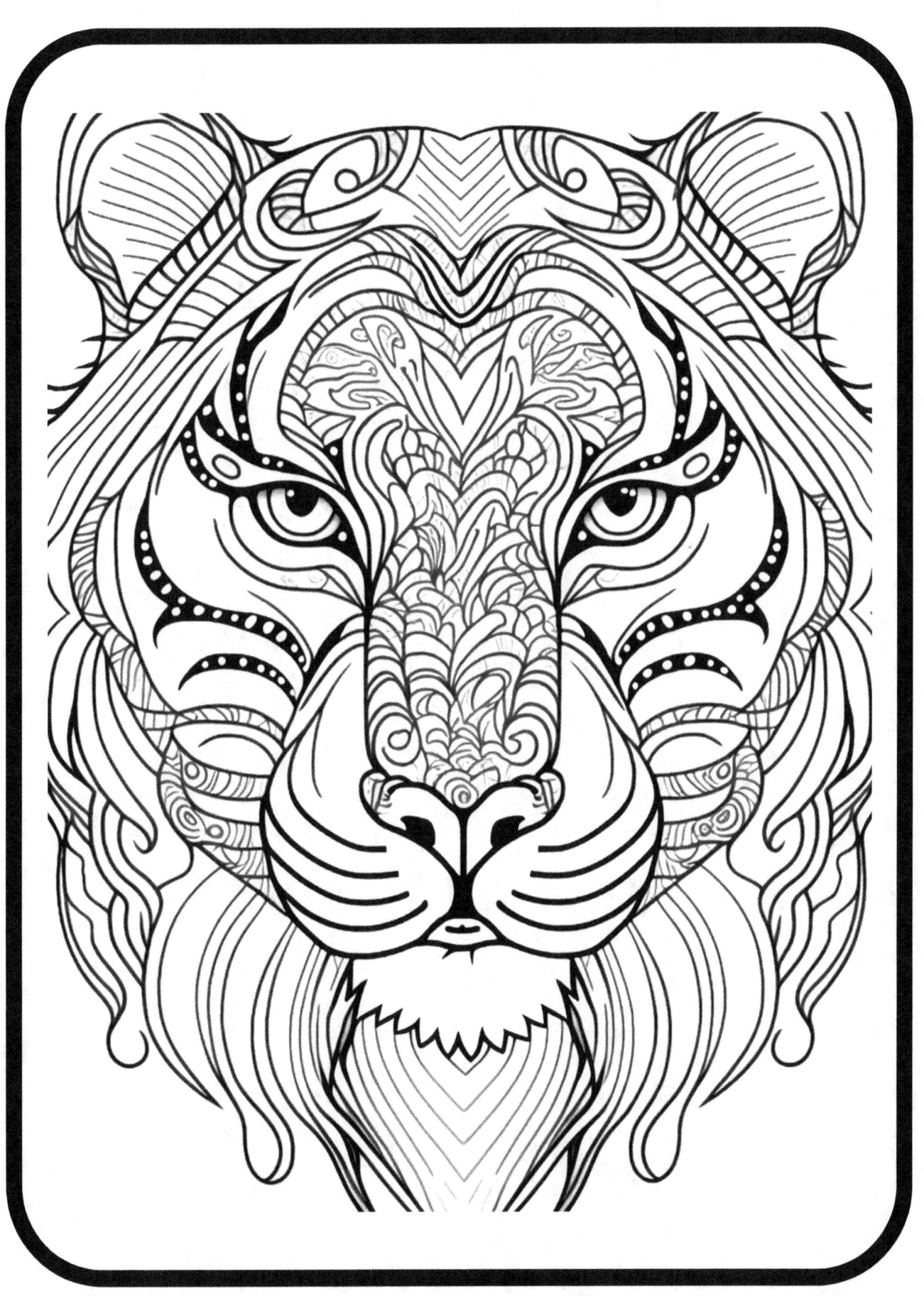

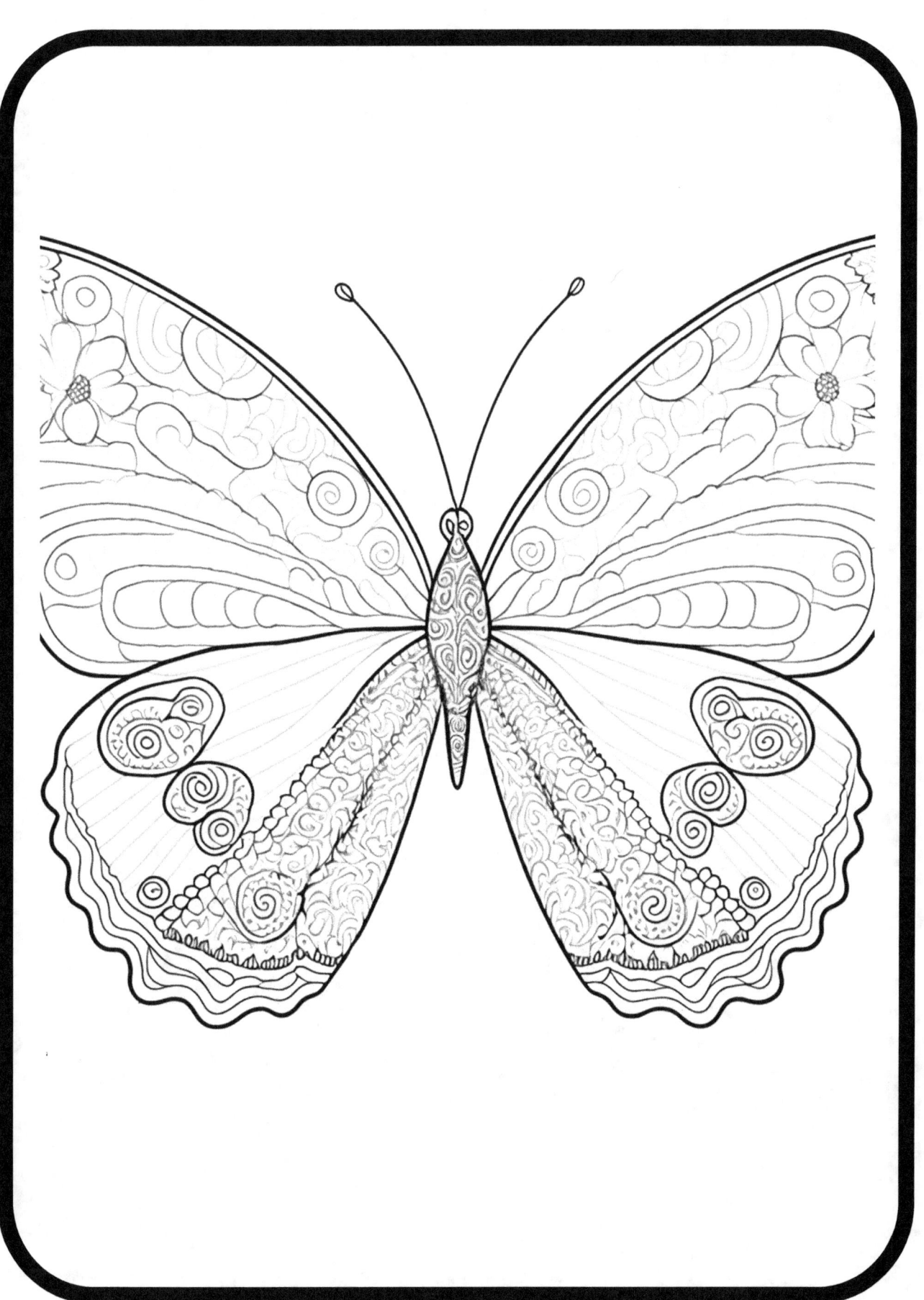

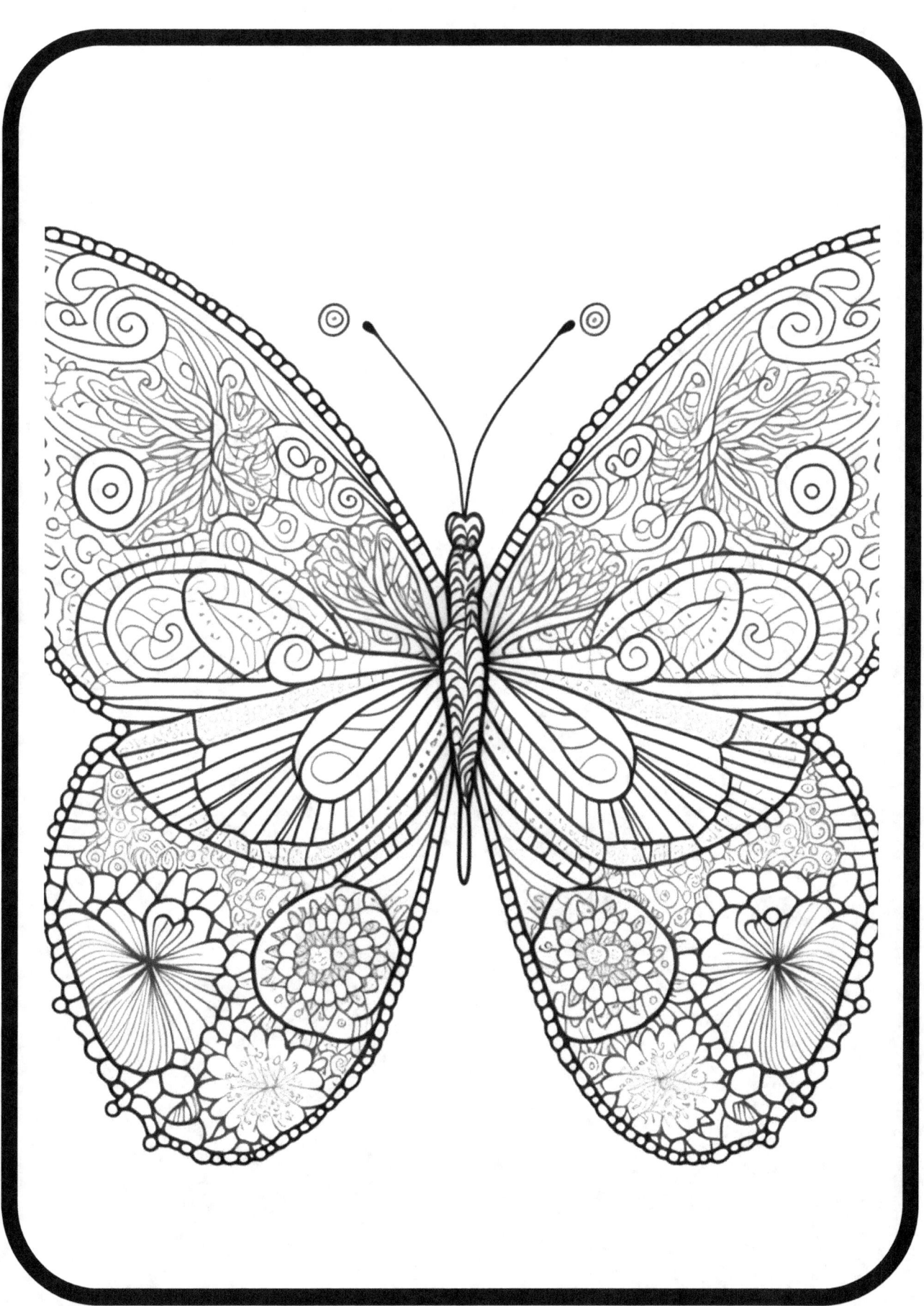

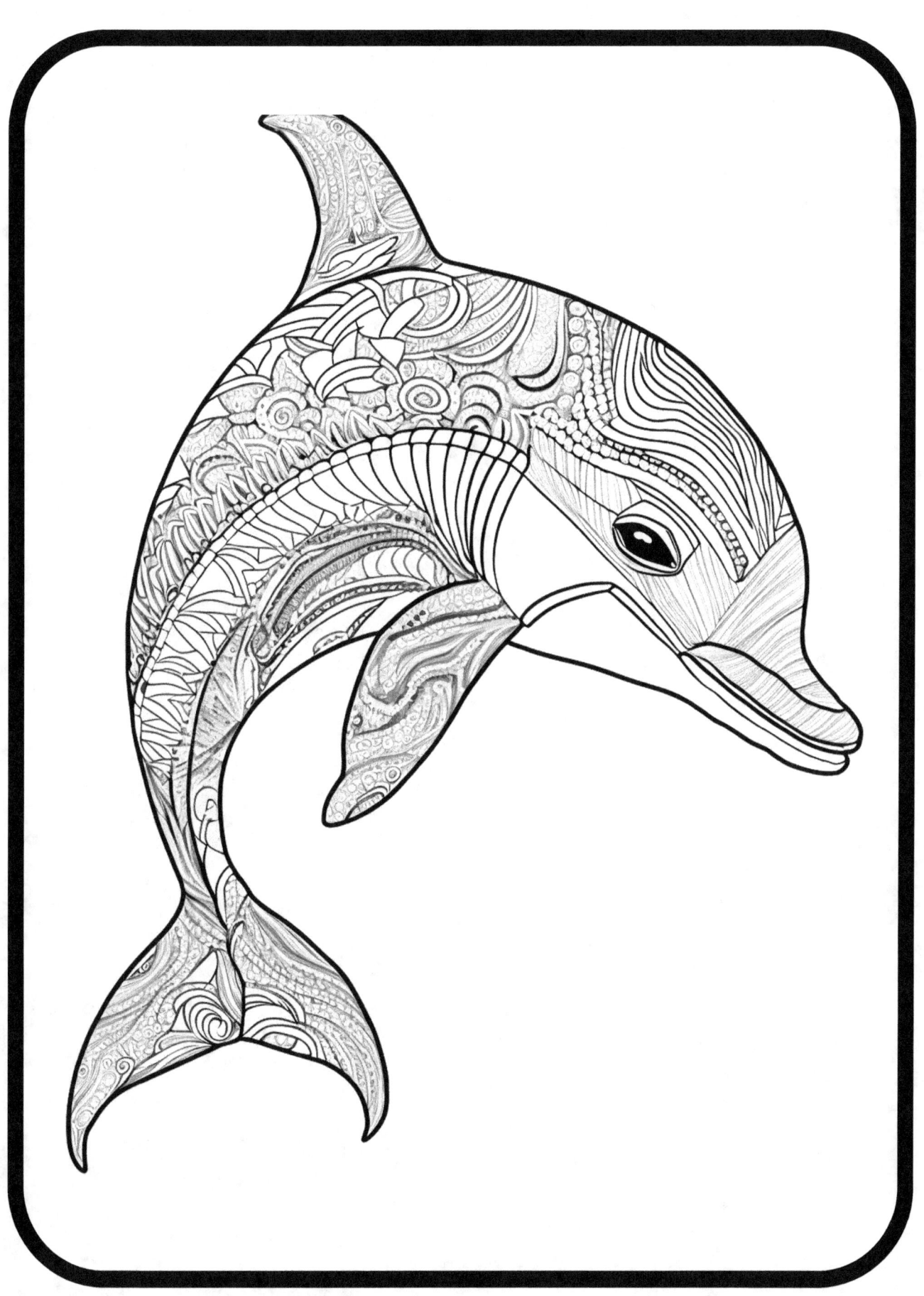

Persistence is key to success.

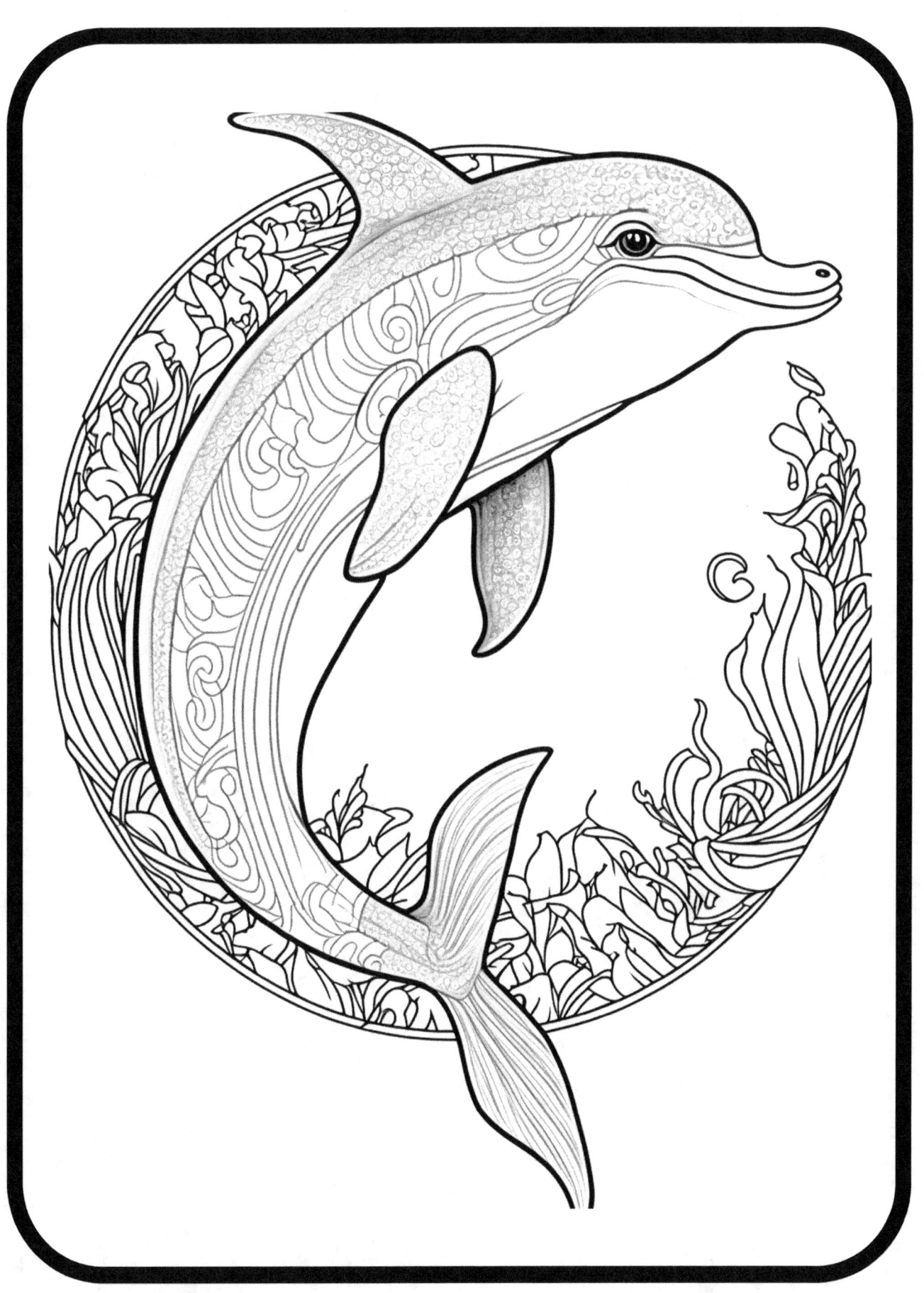

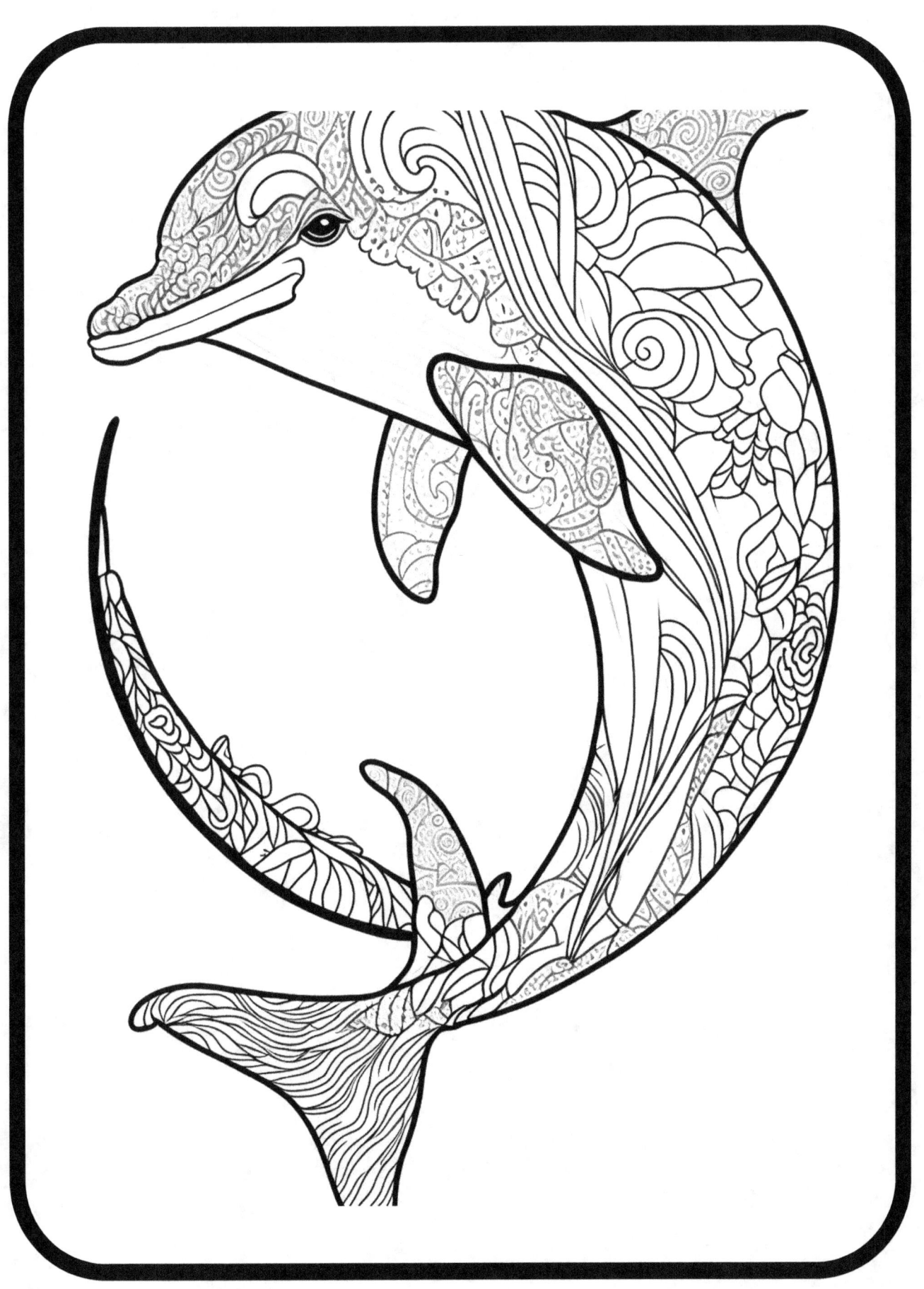

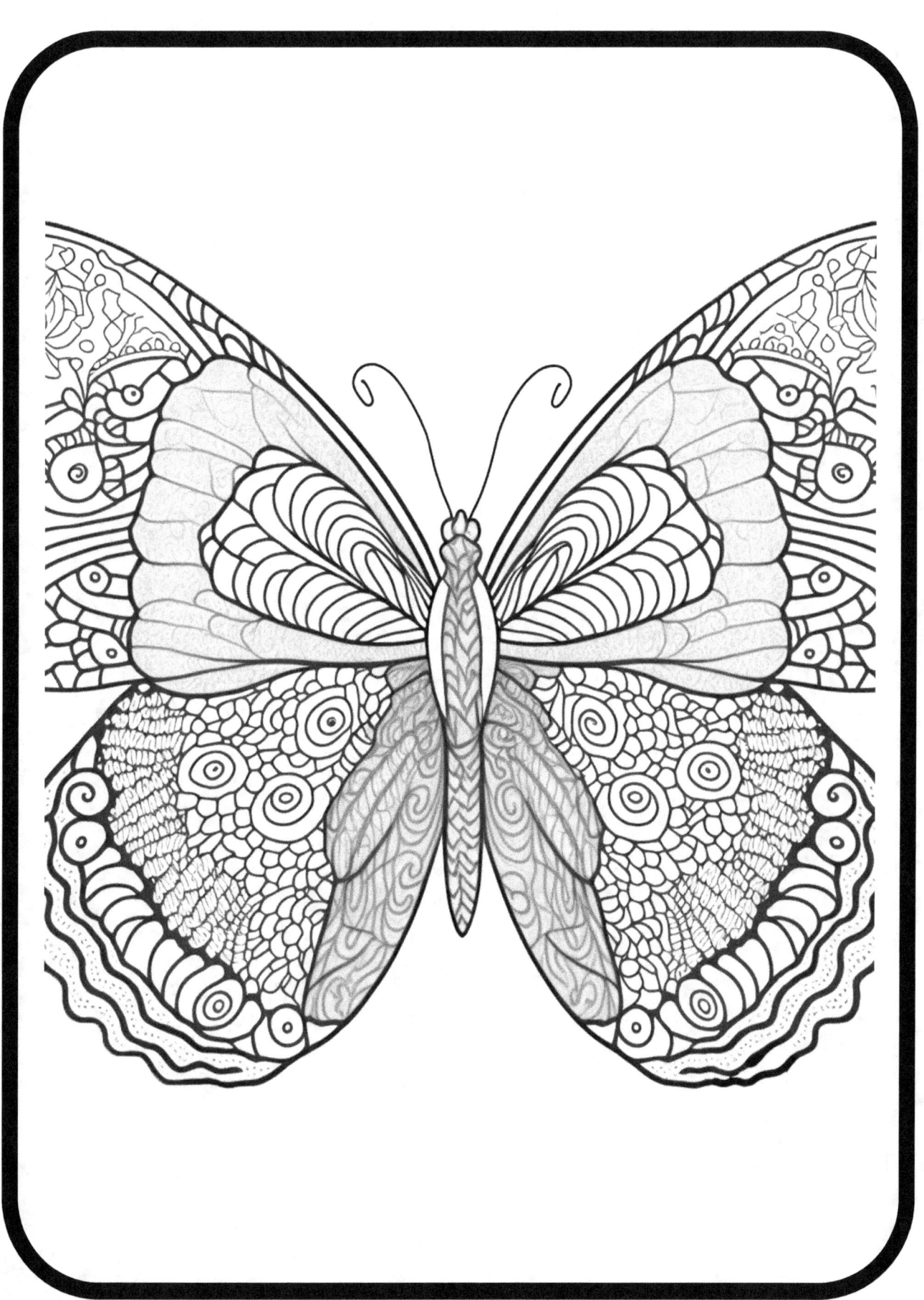

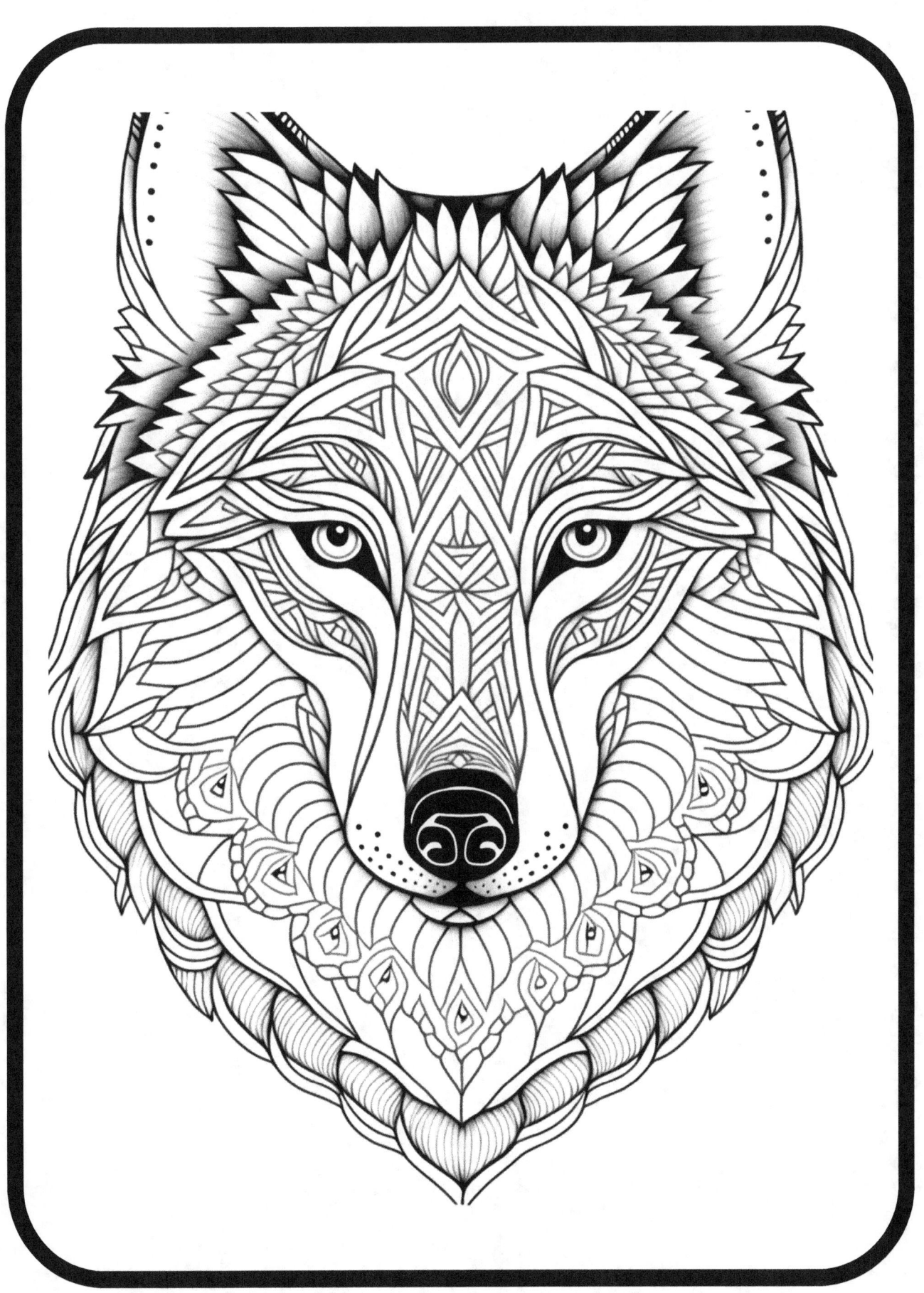

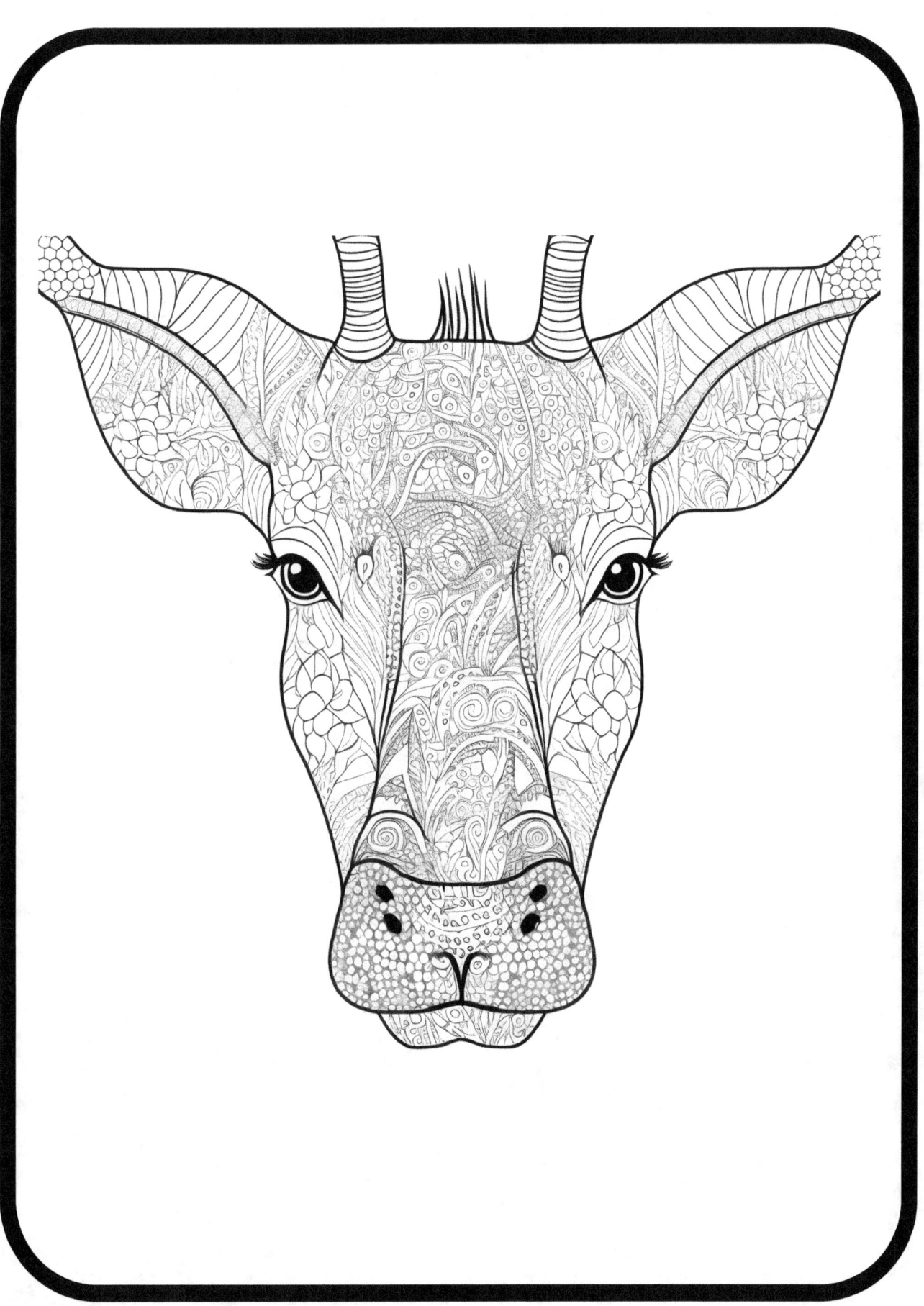

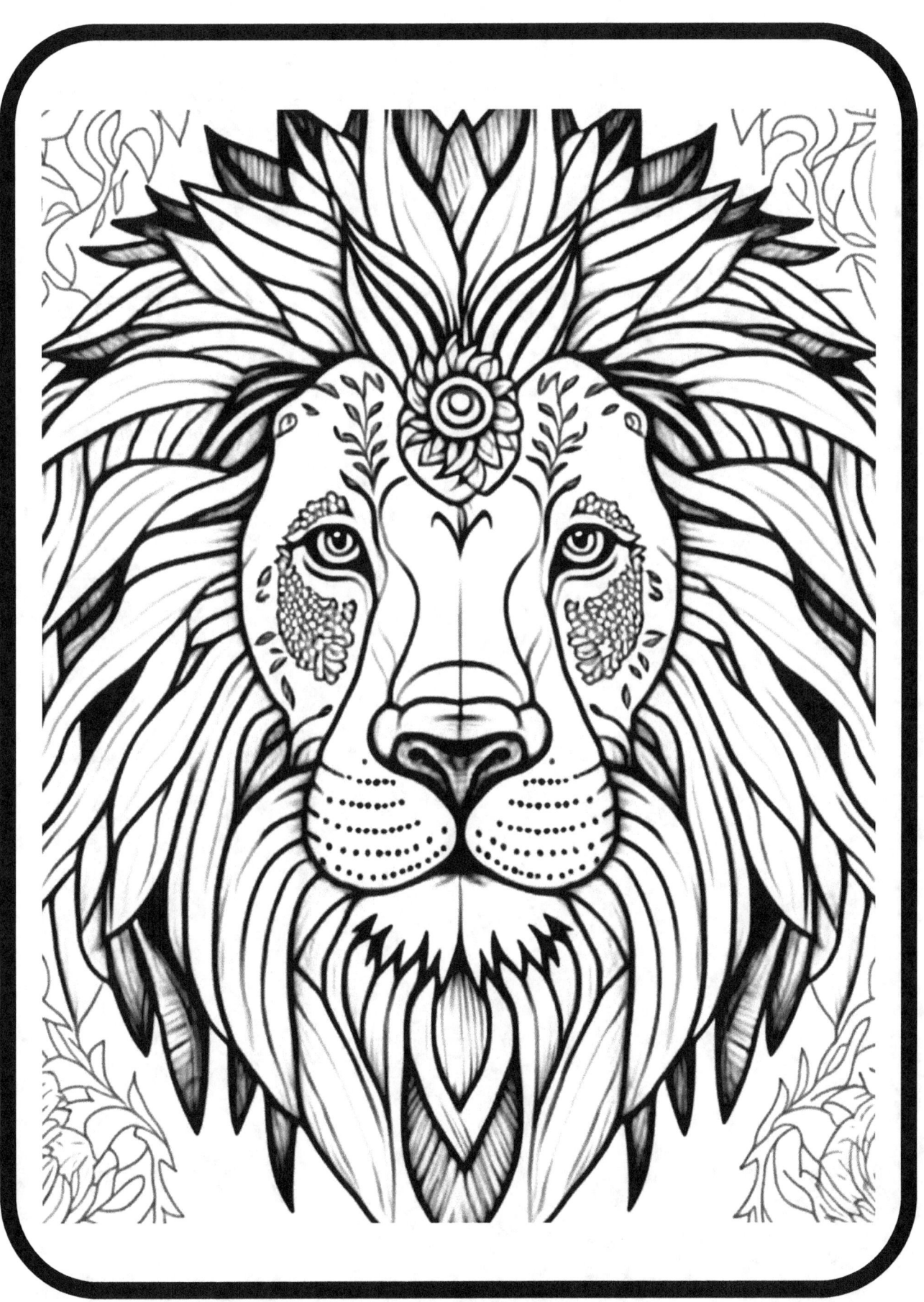

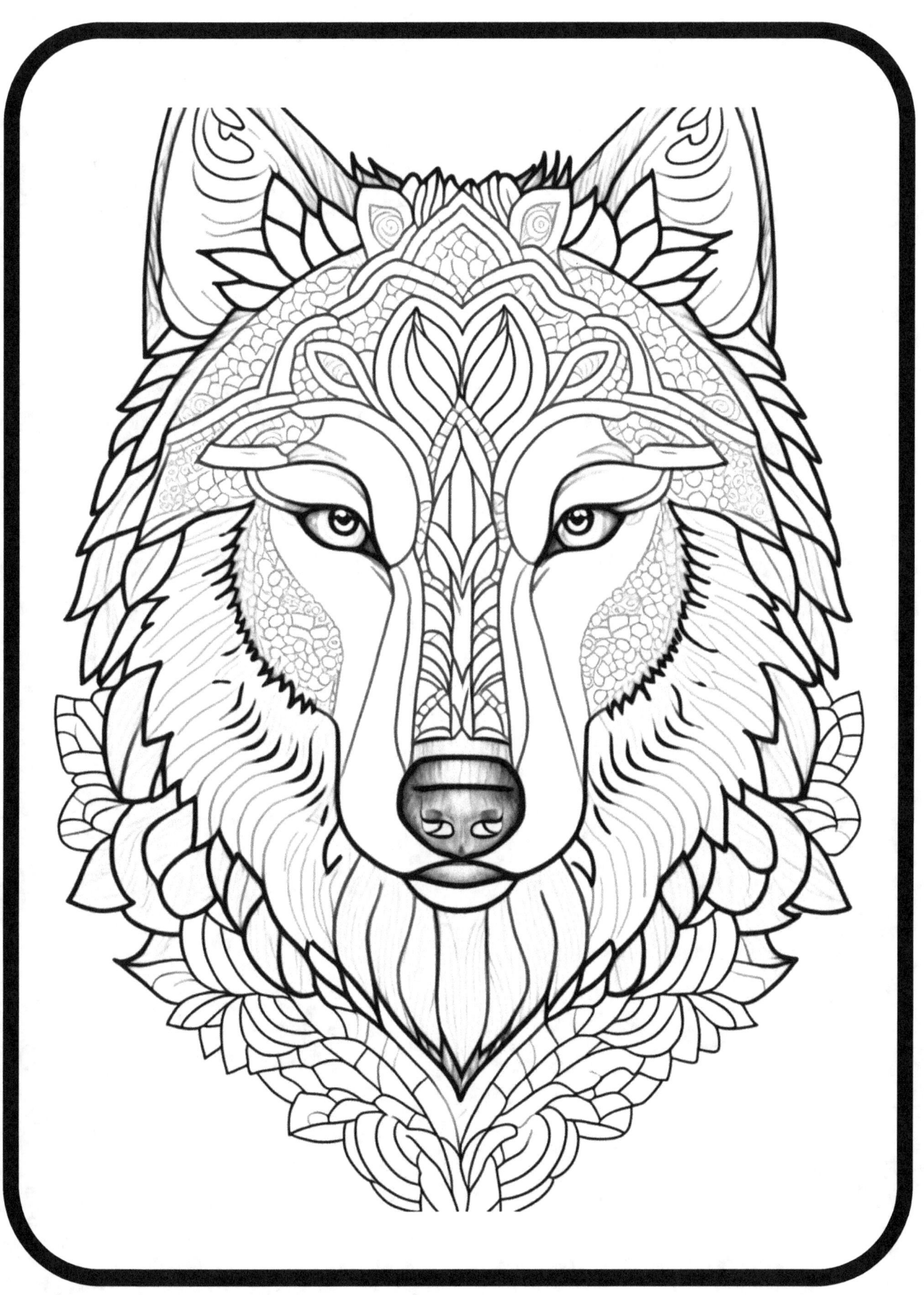

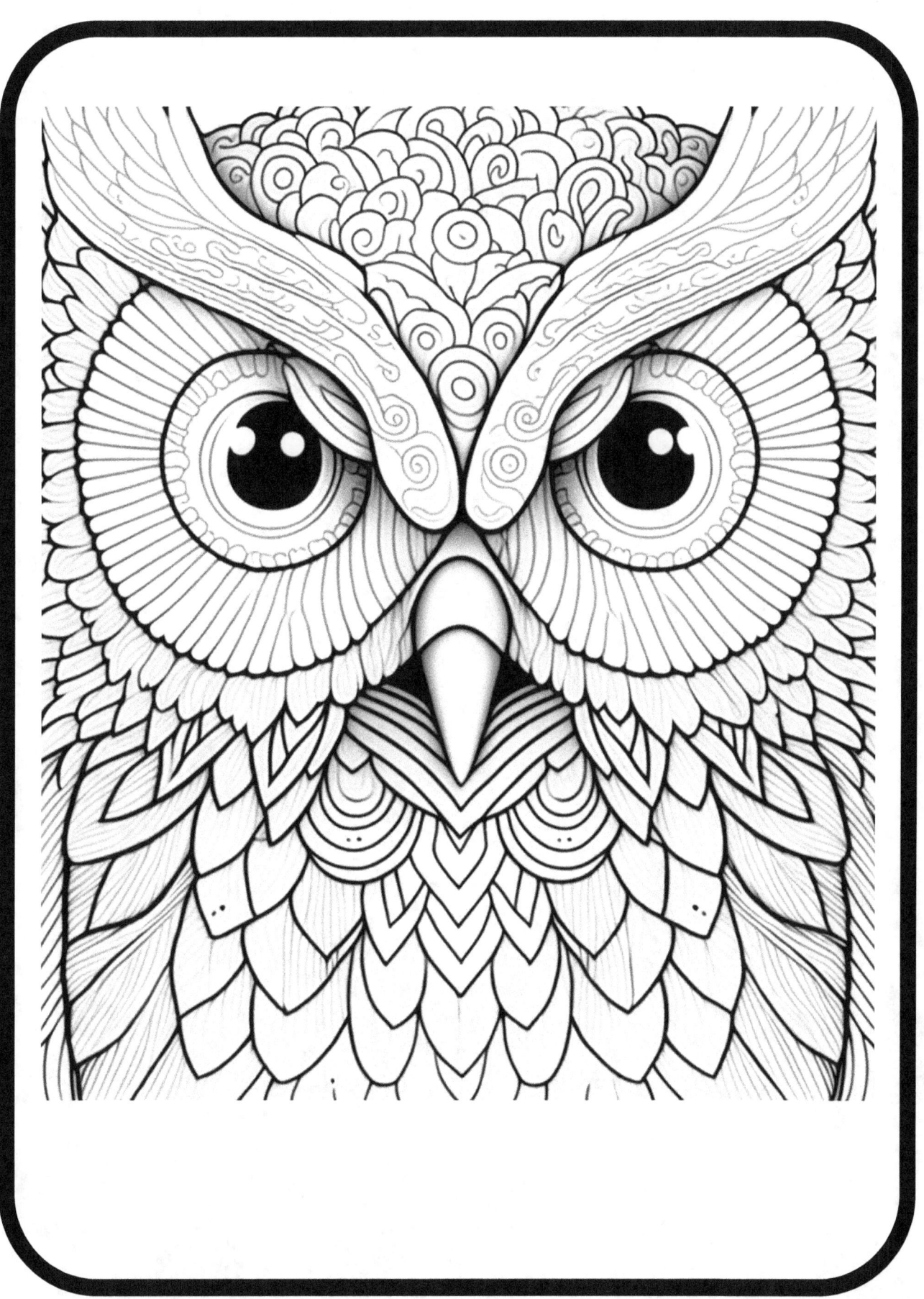

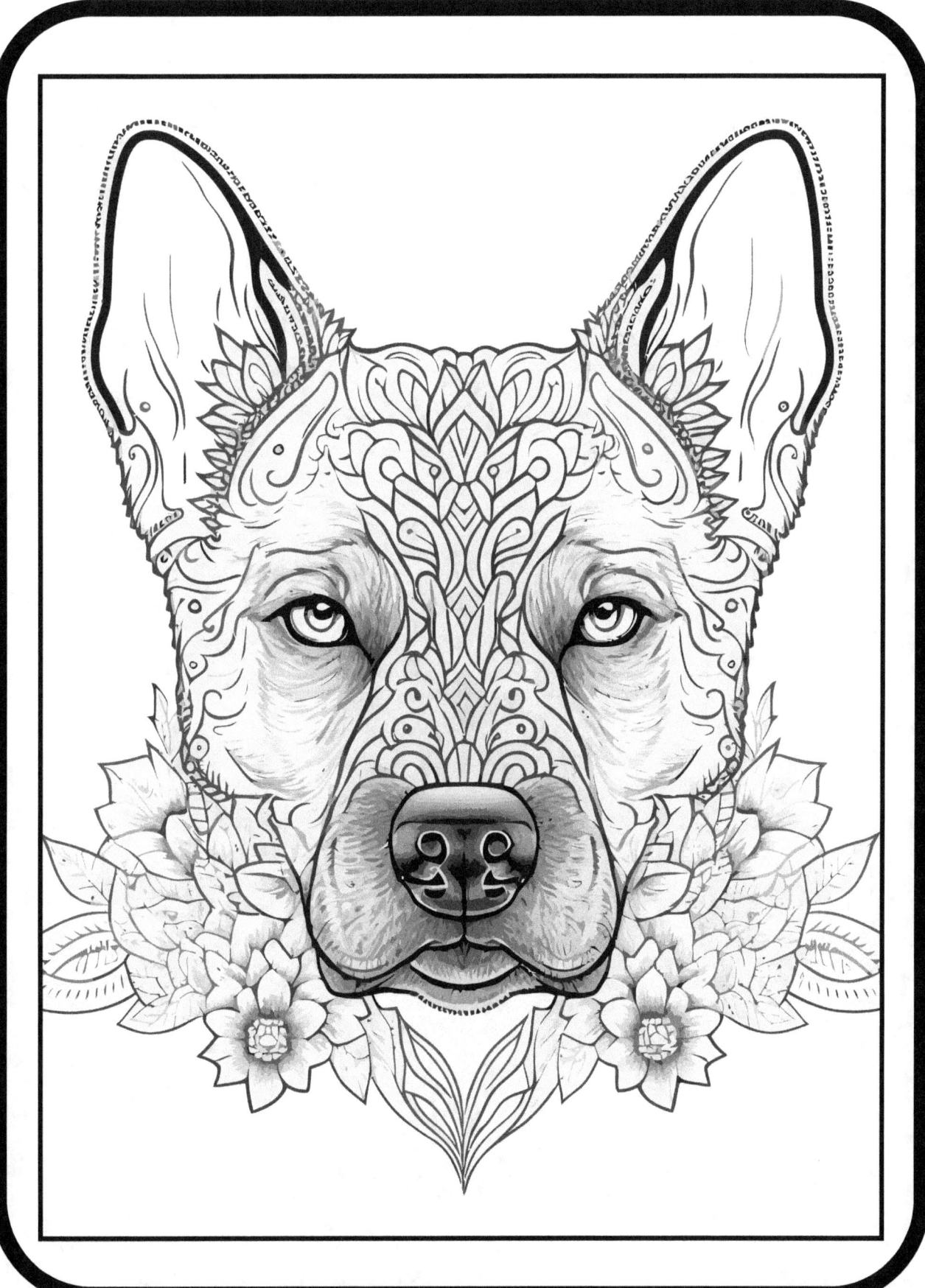

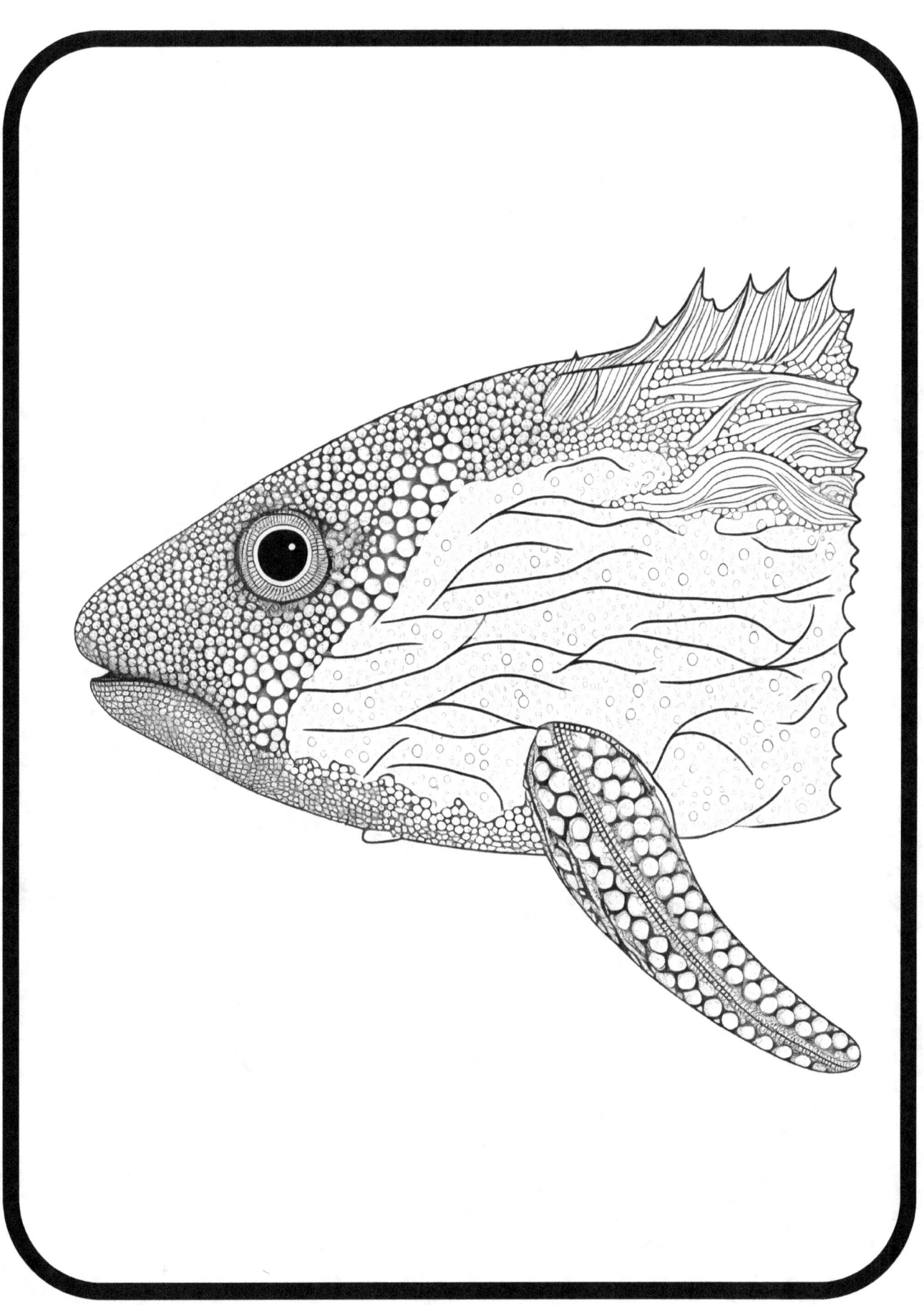

Every day is a new chance.

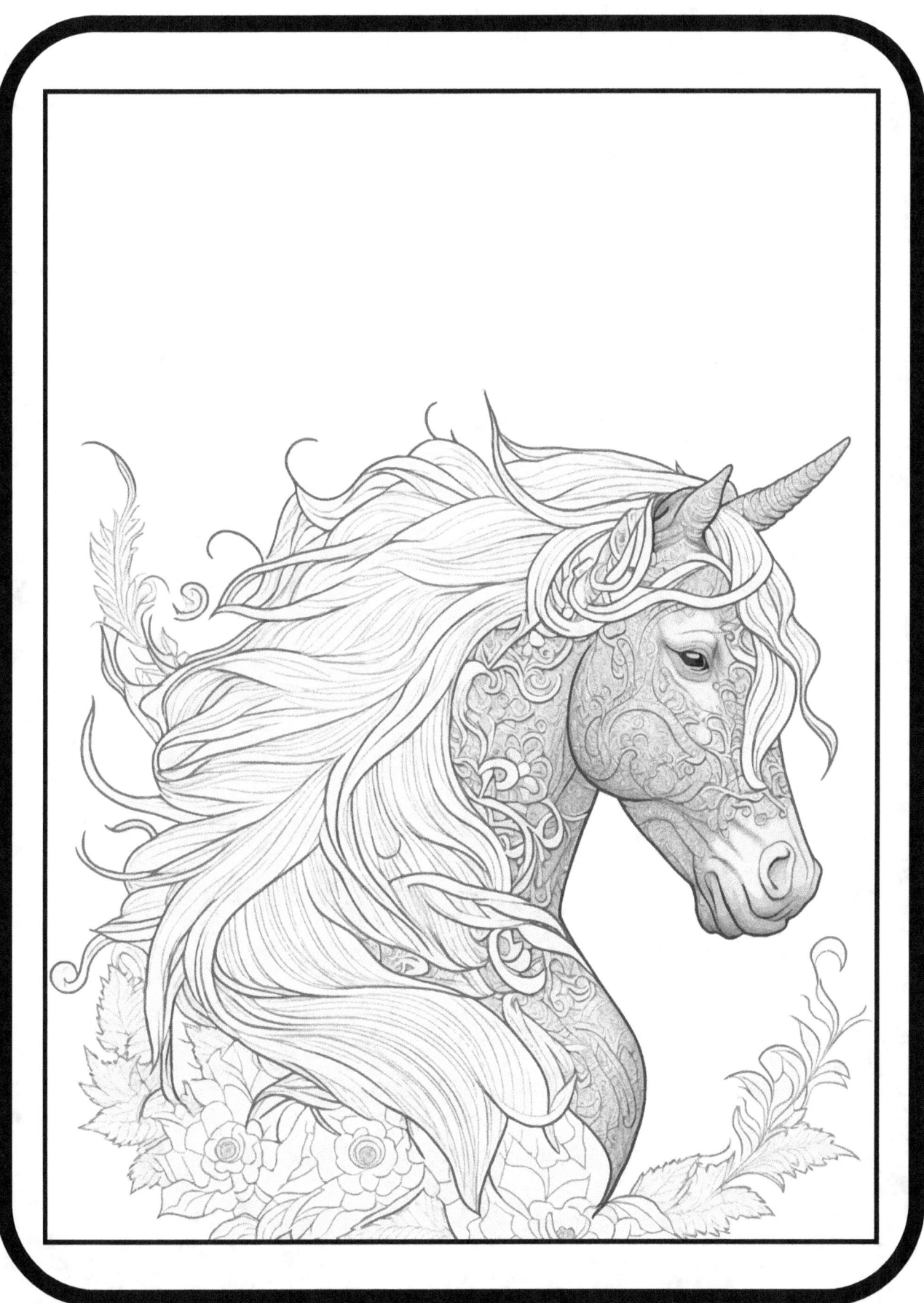

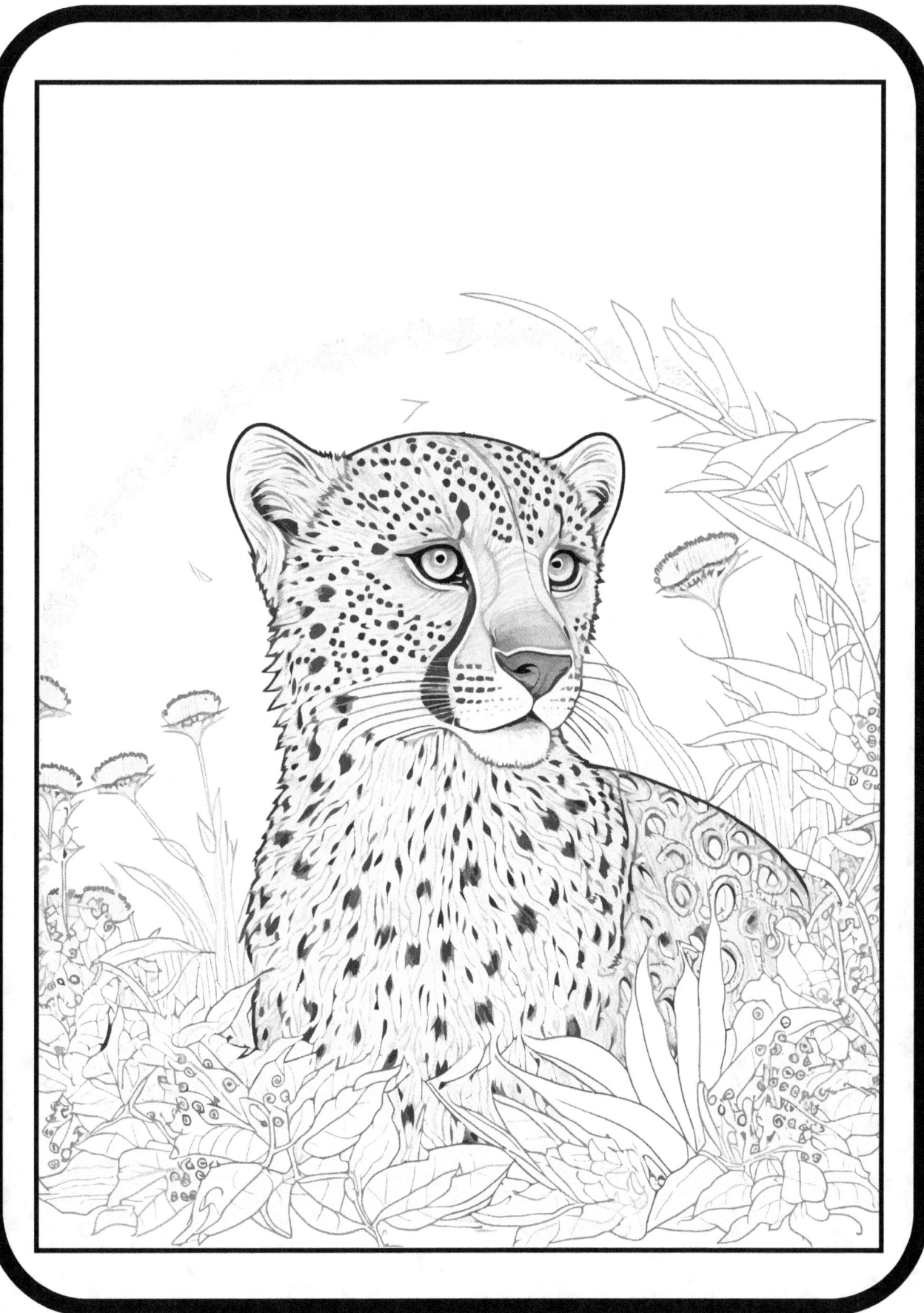

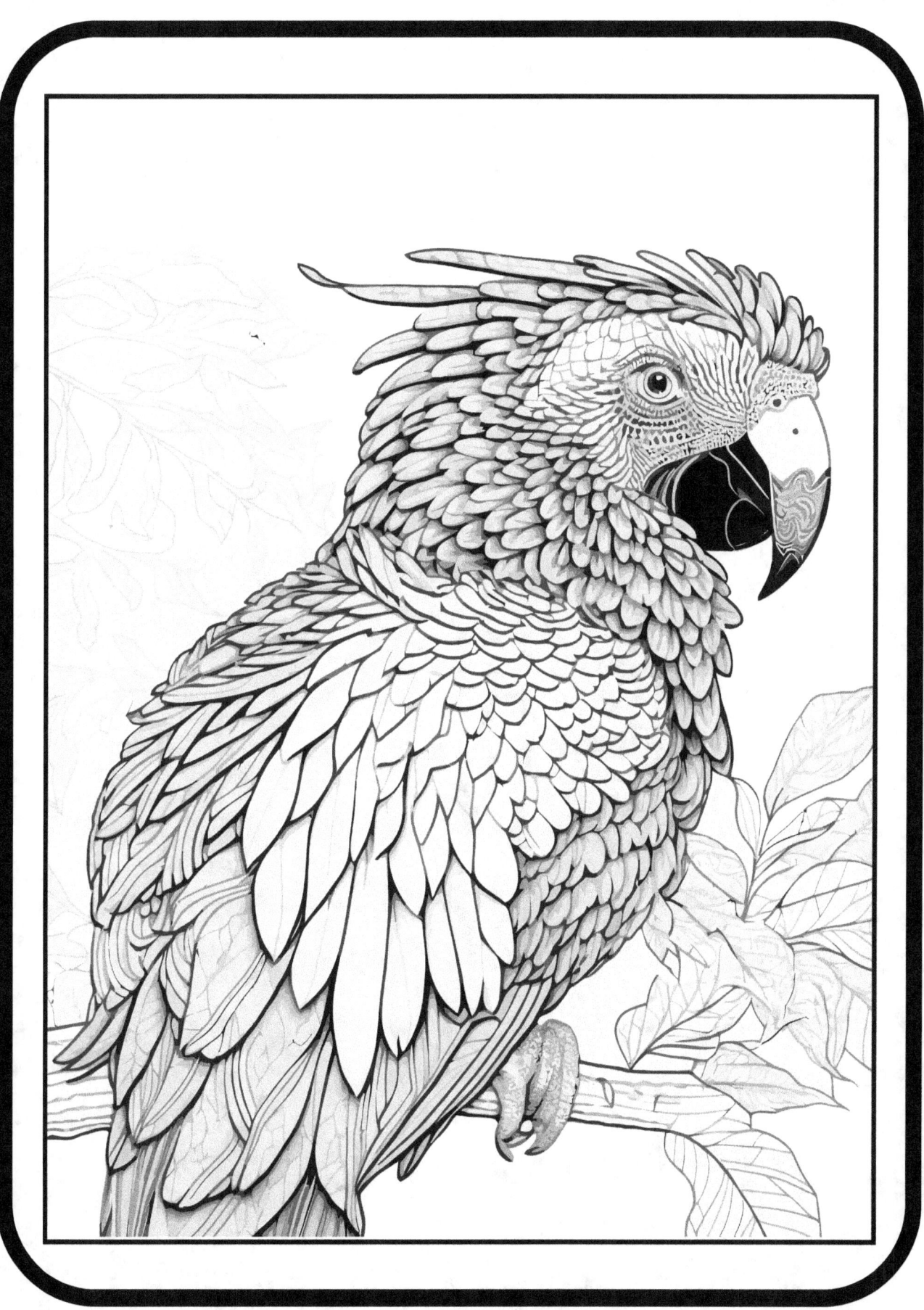

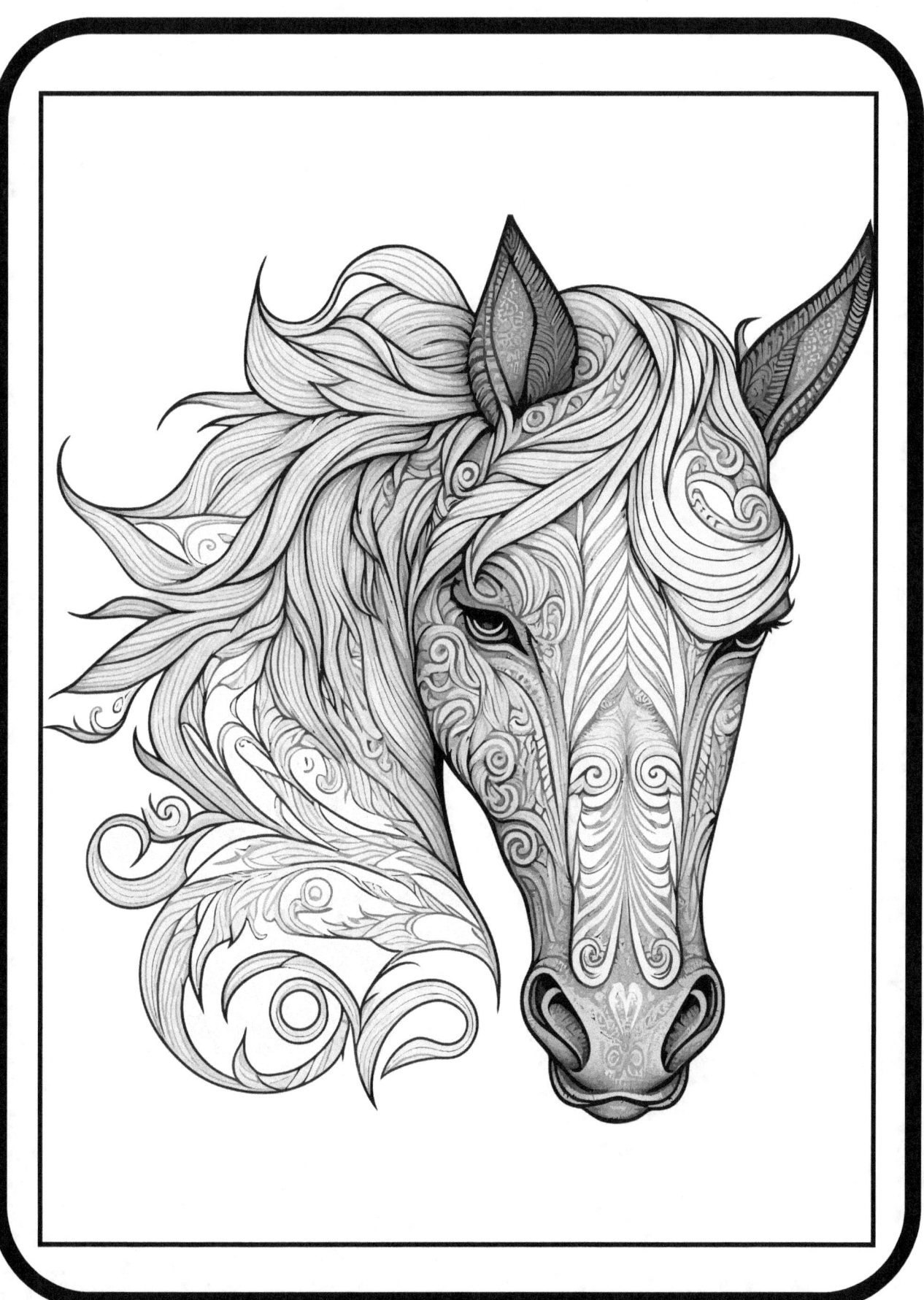

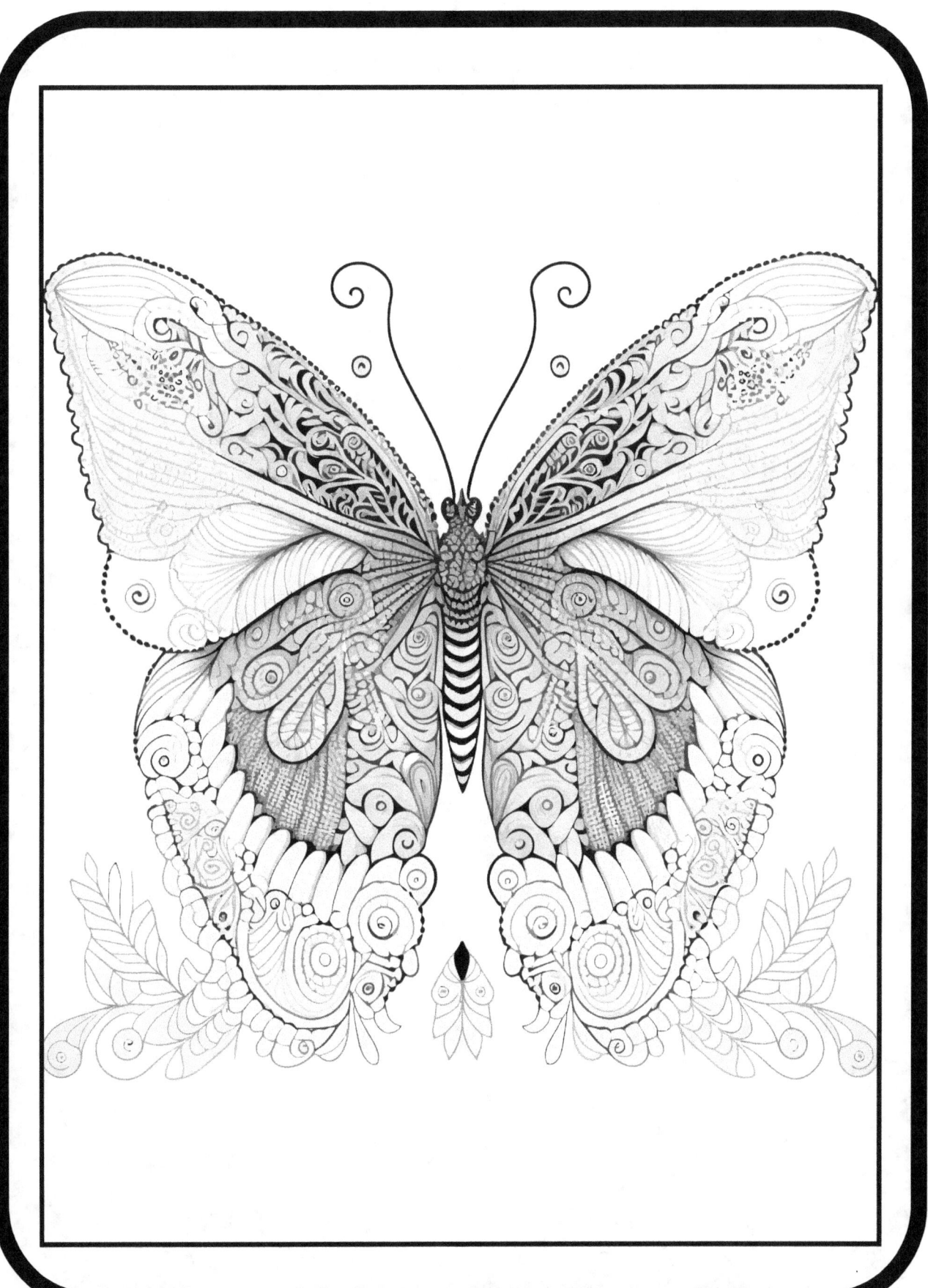

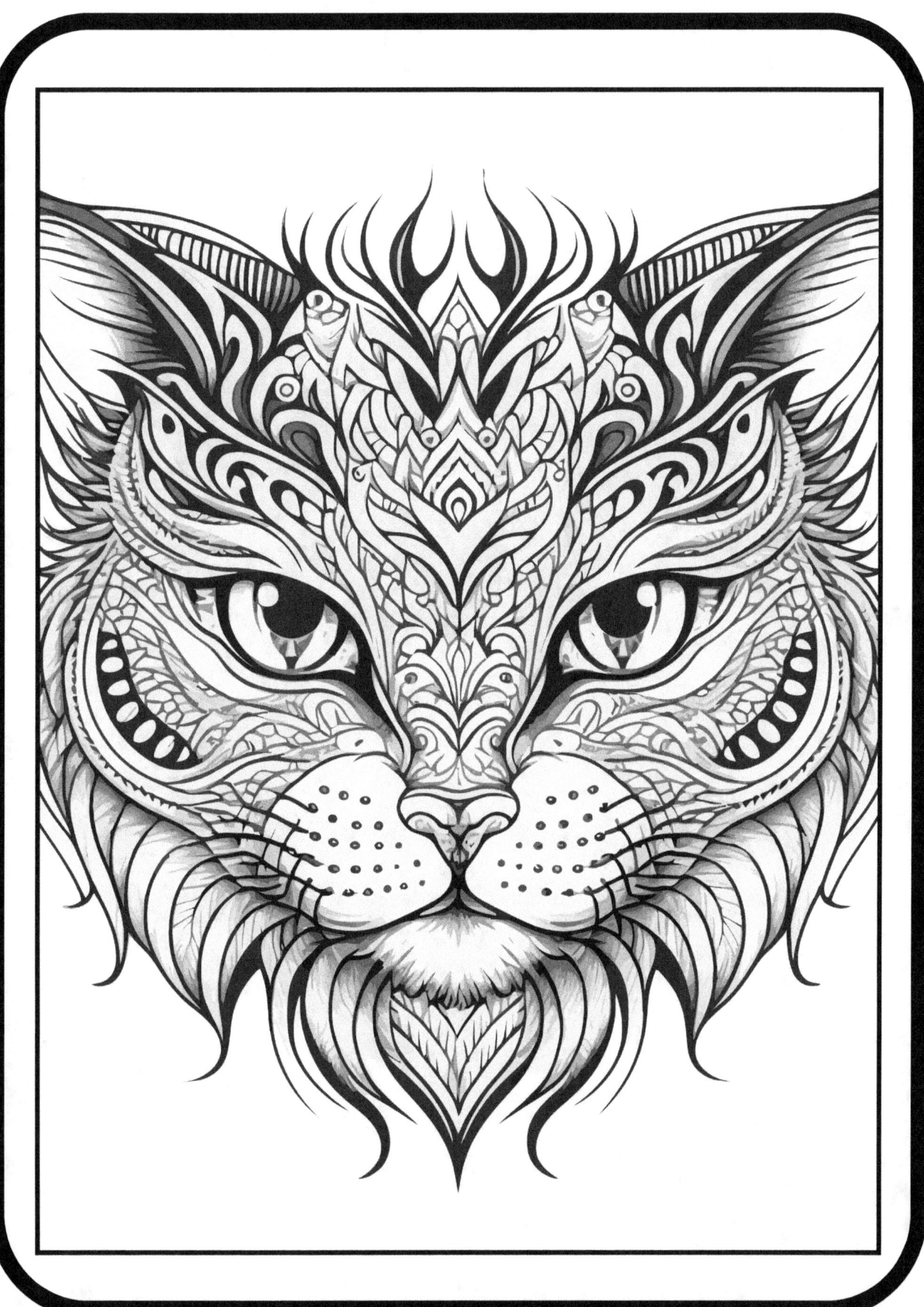

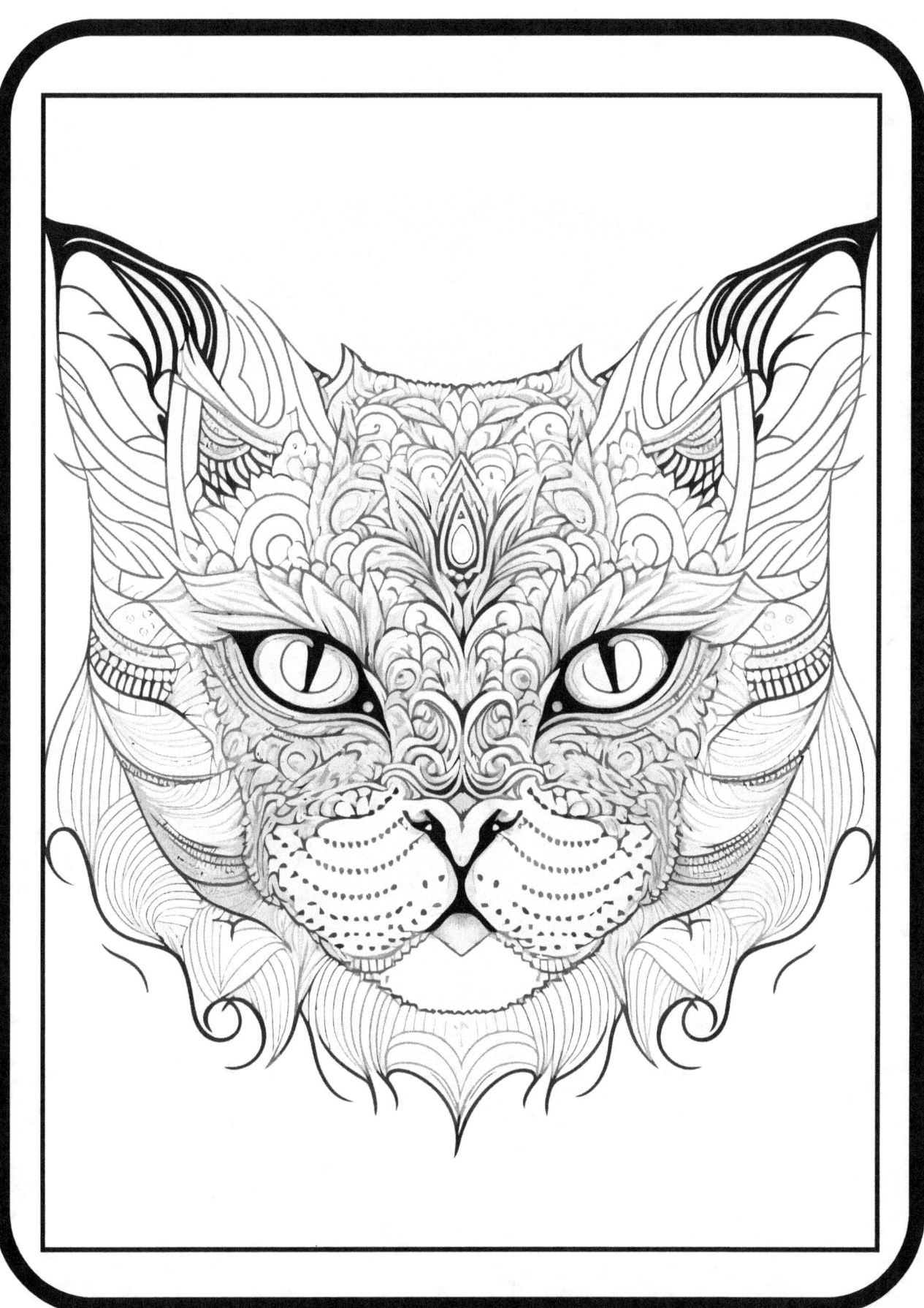

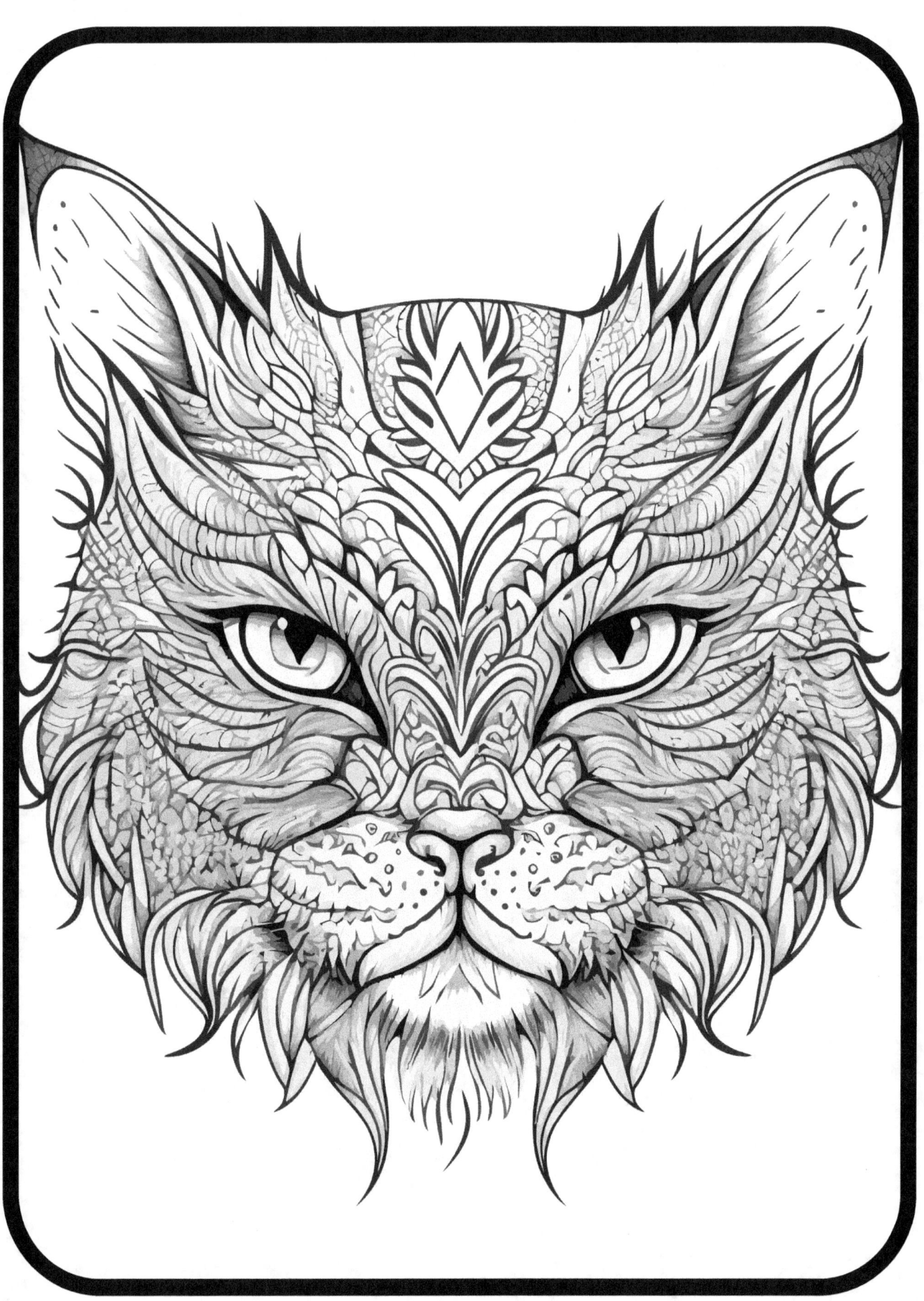

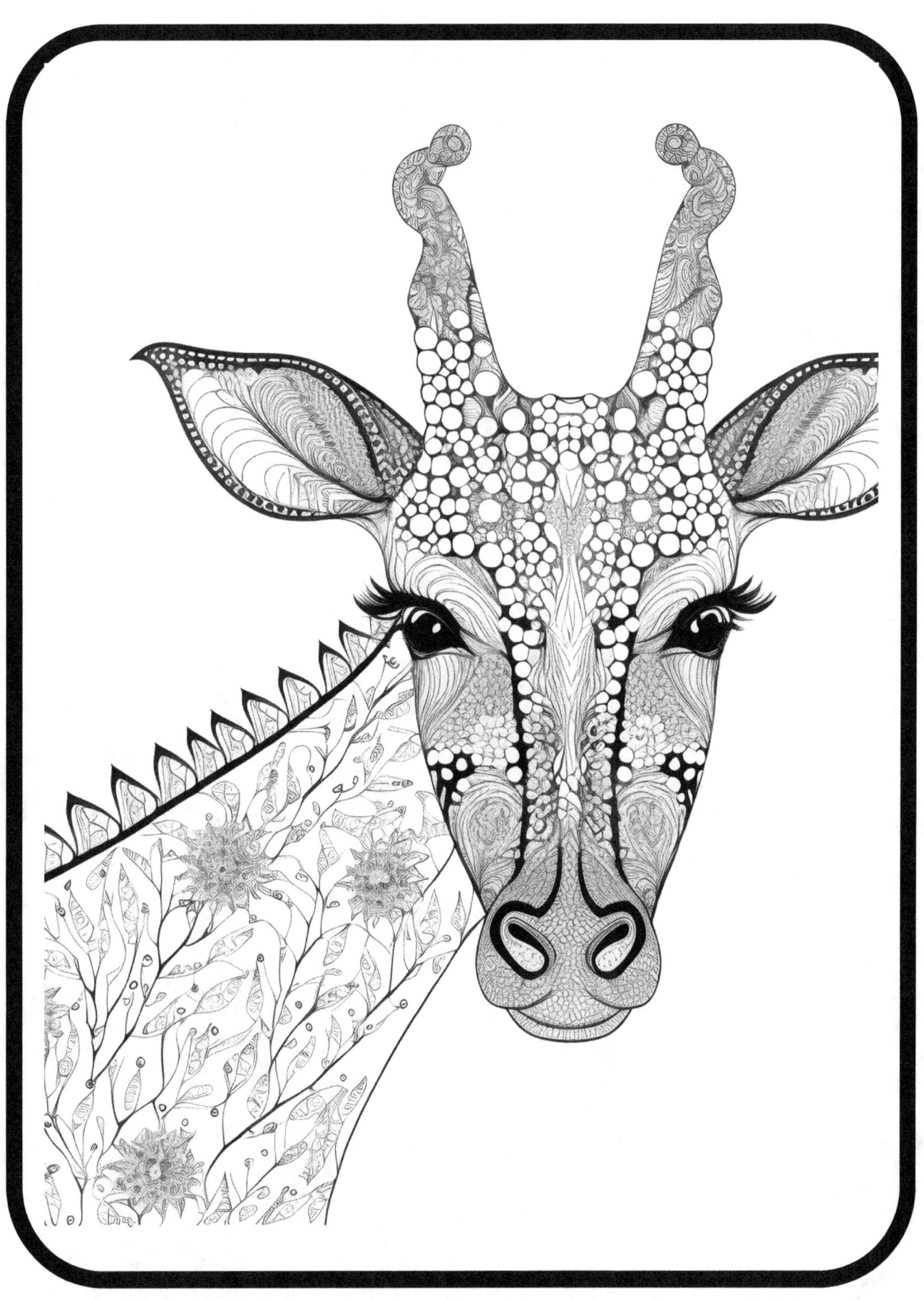

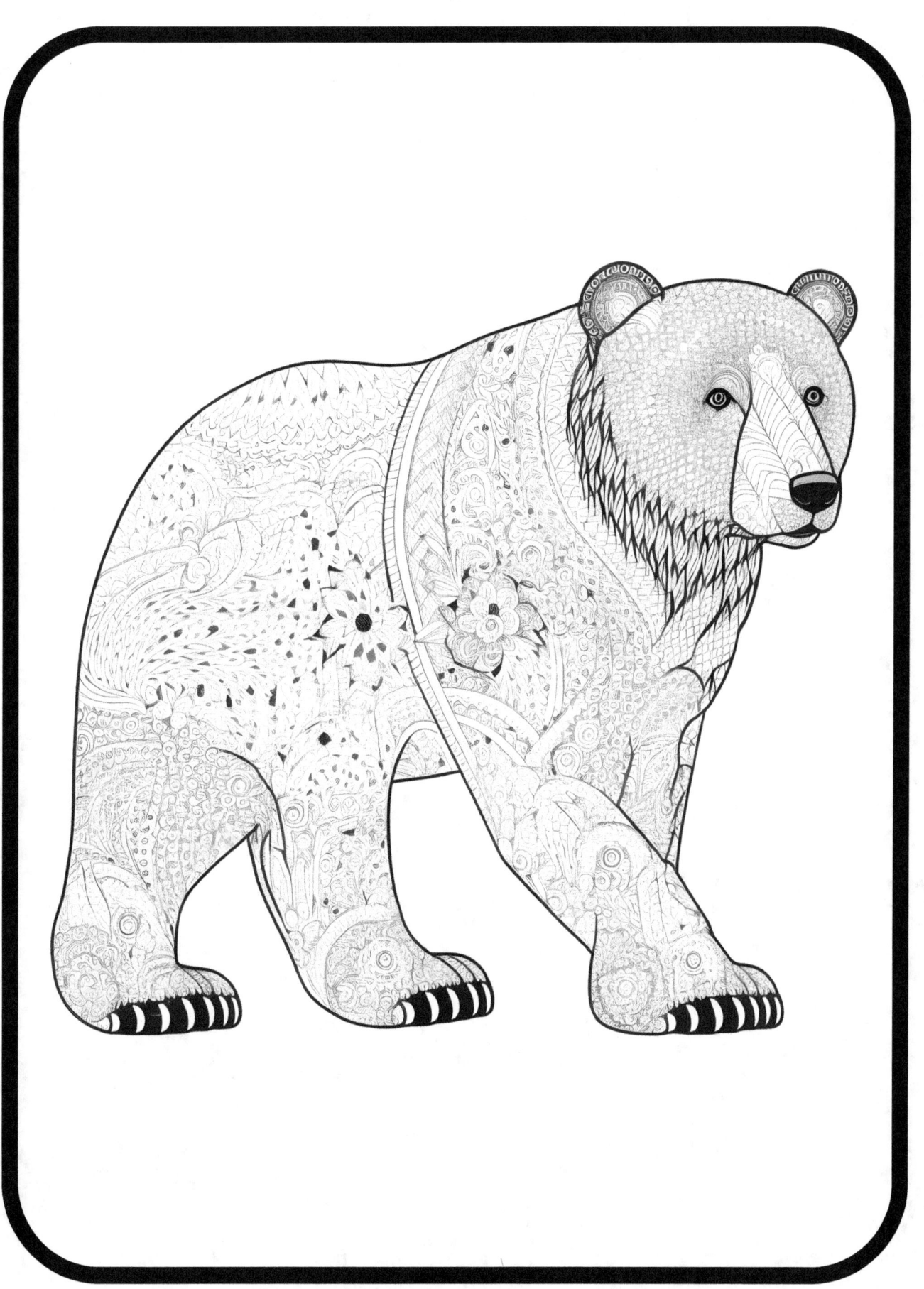

Take the first step.

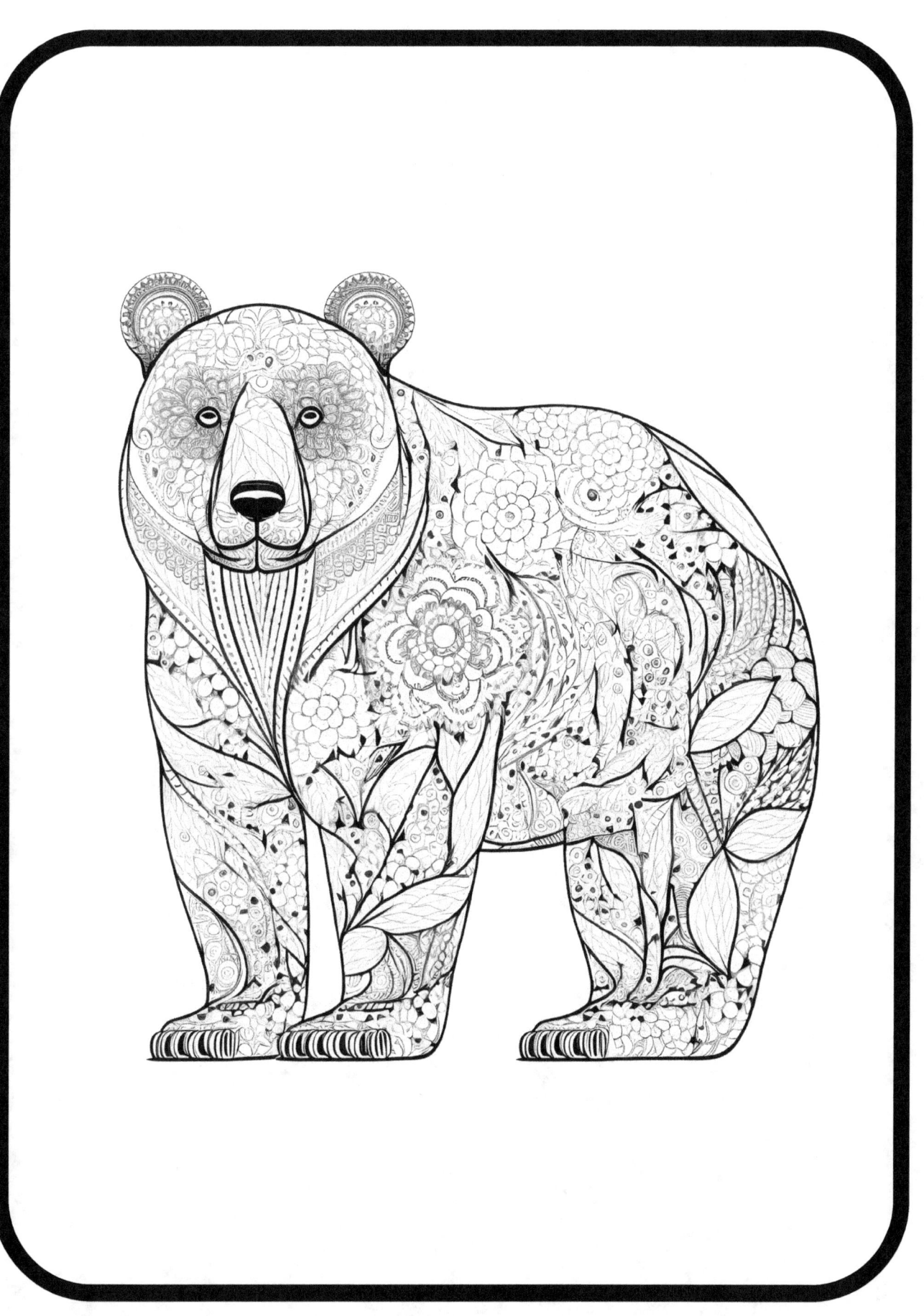

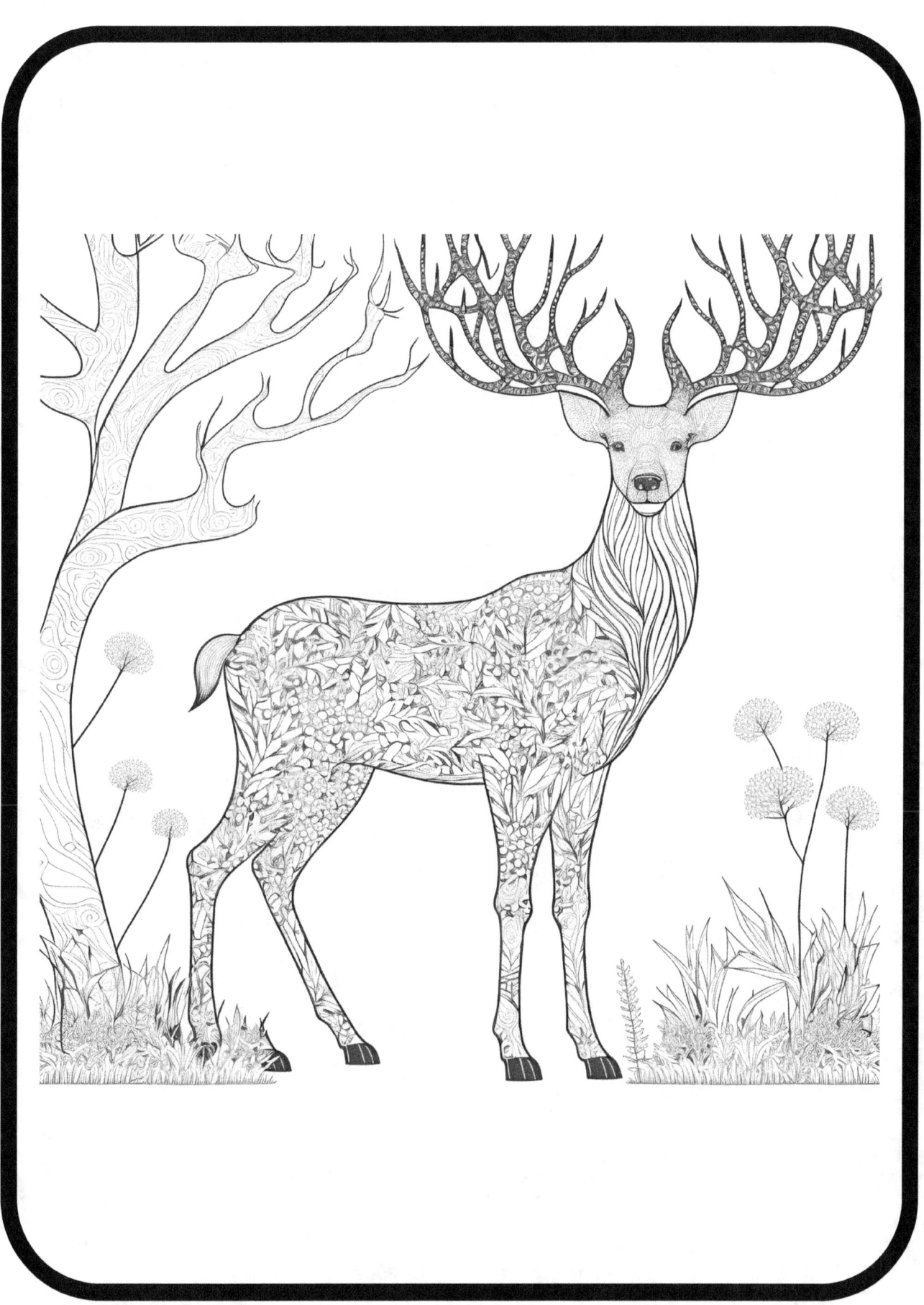

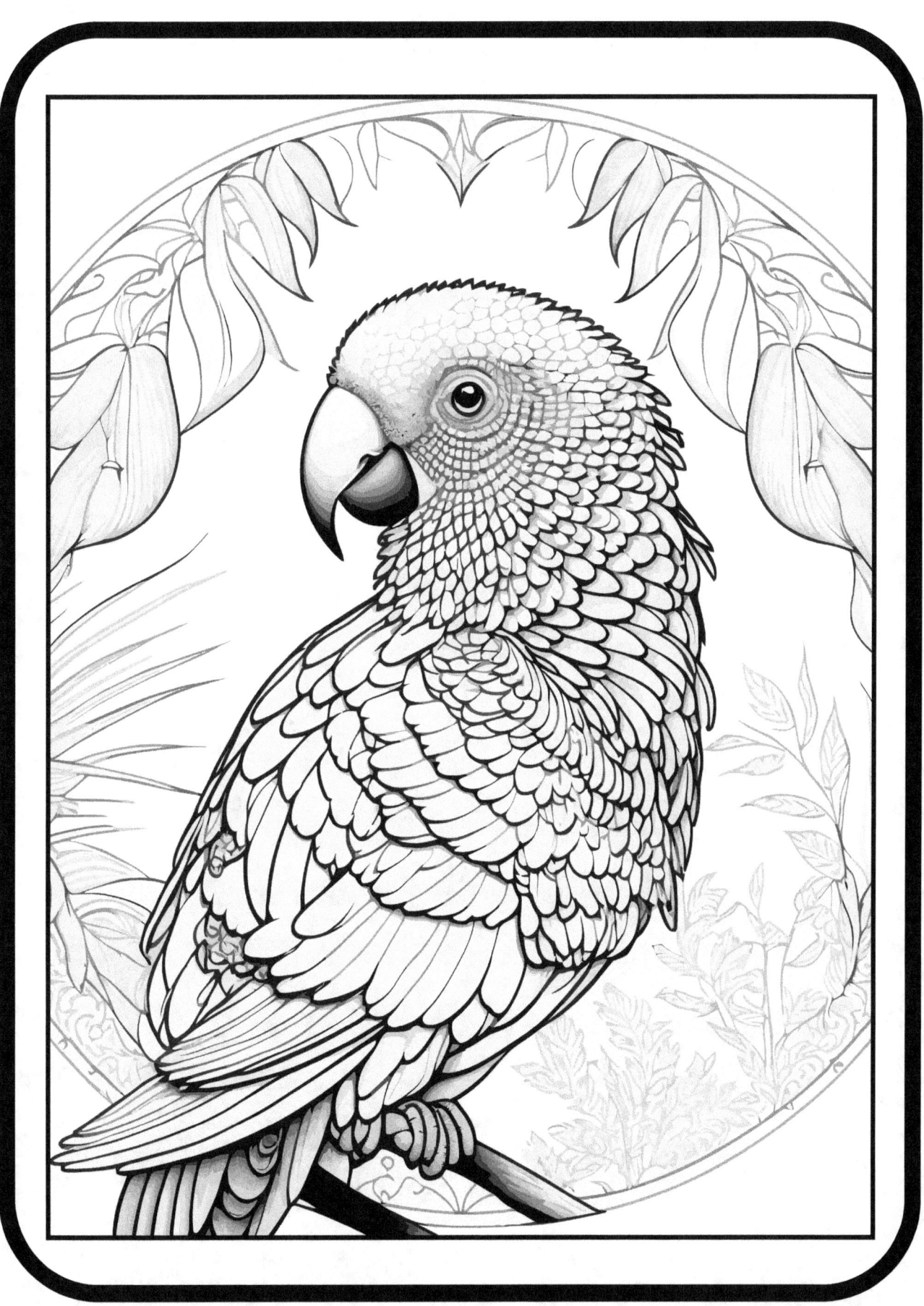

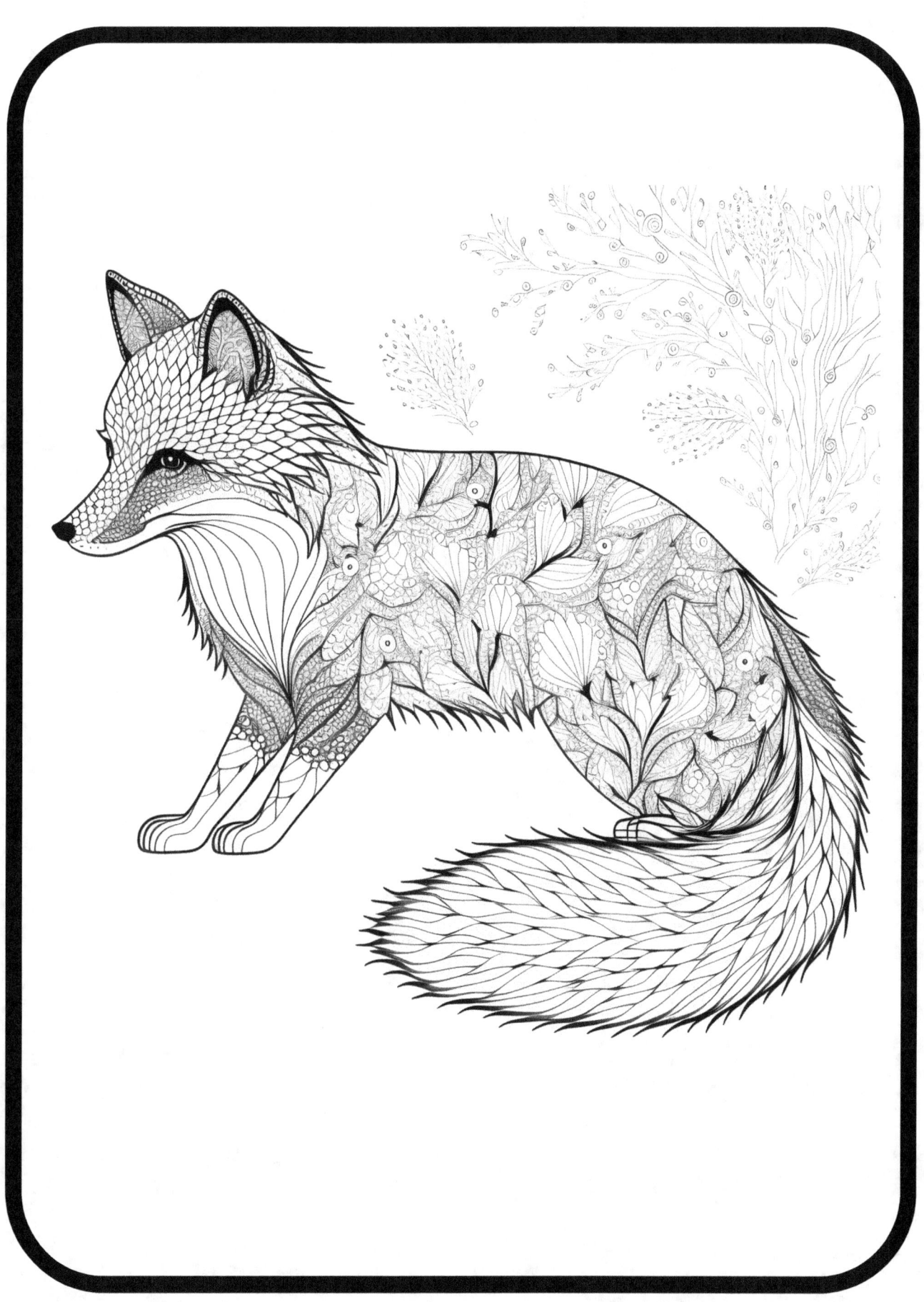

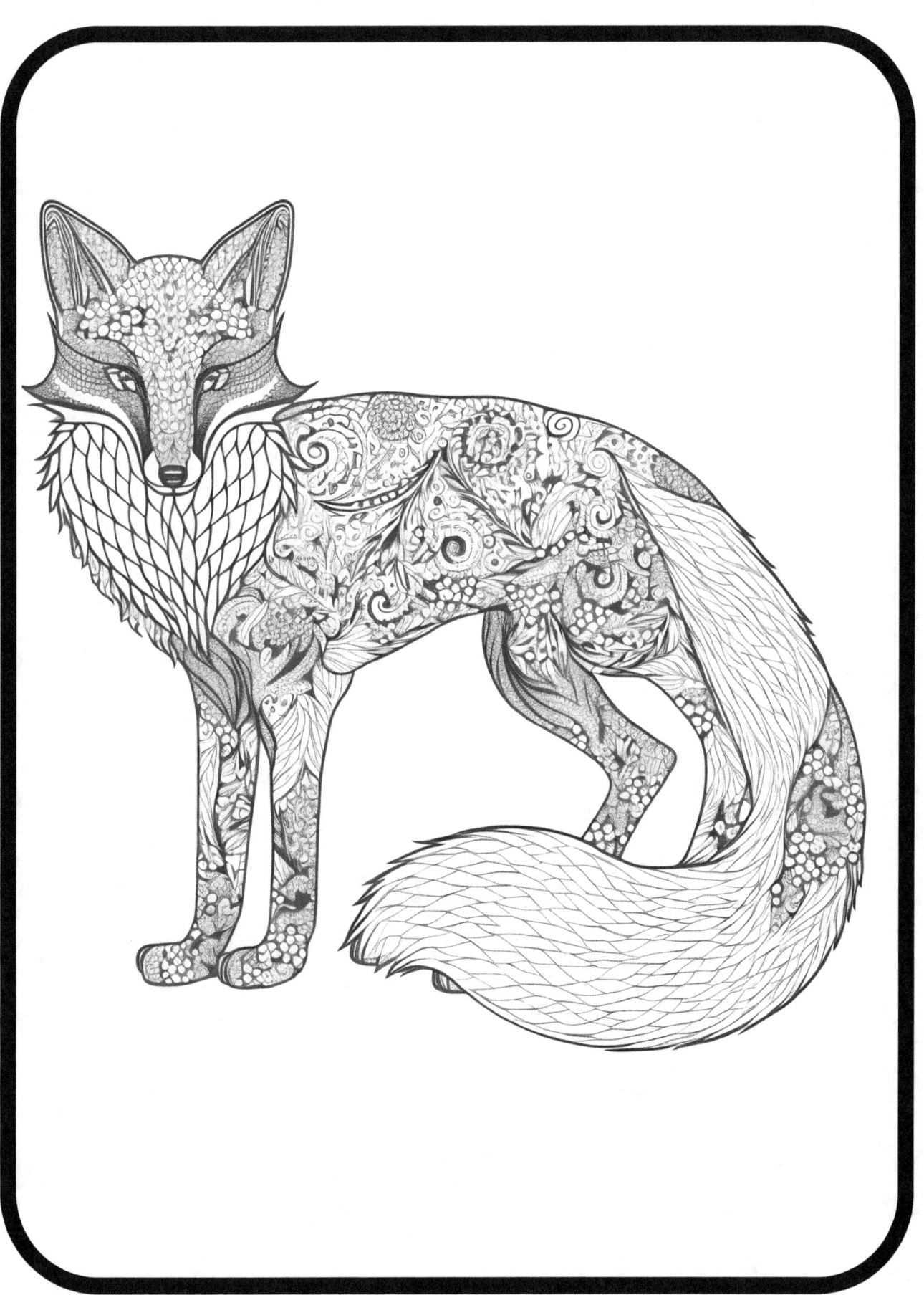

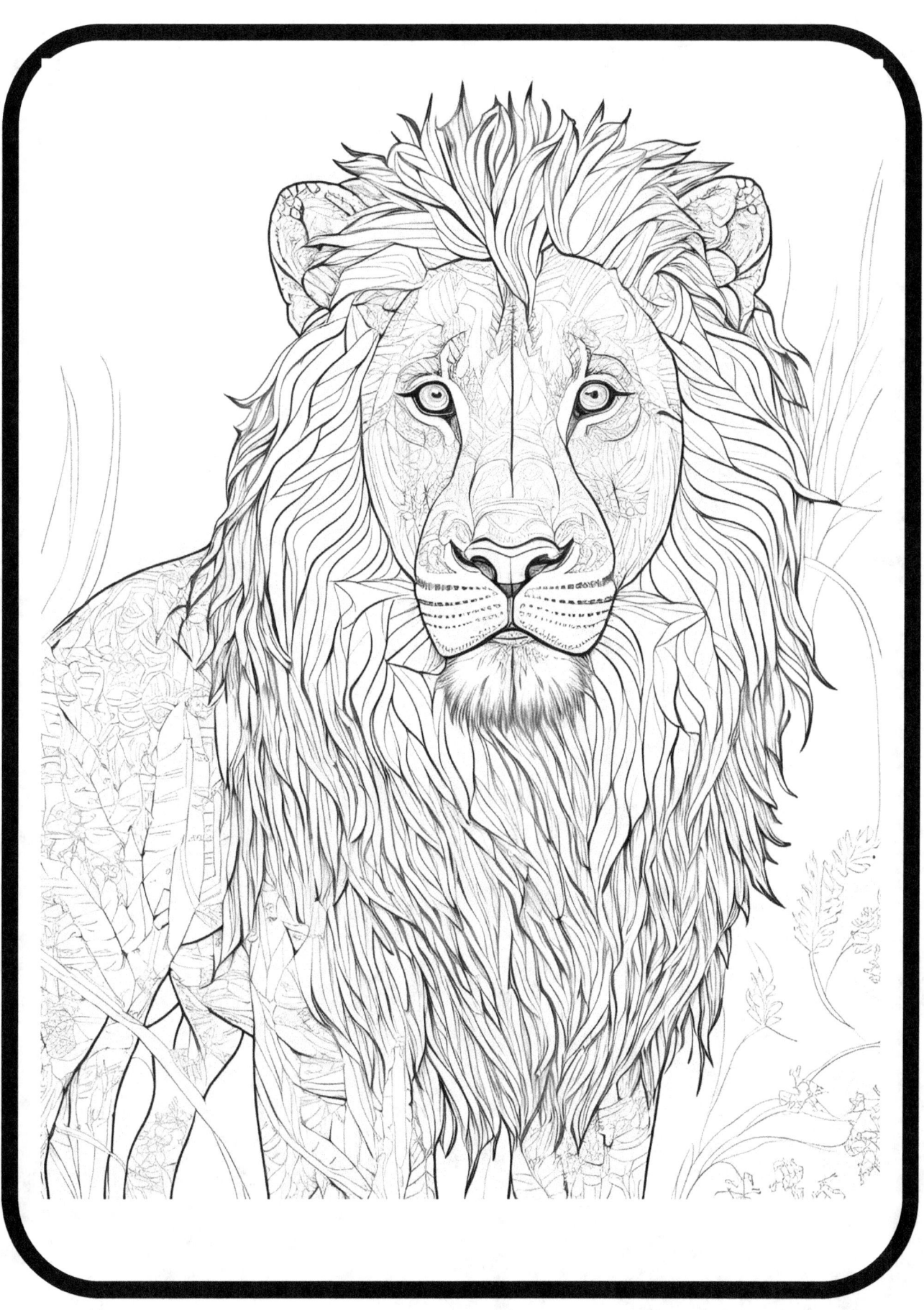

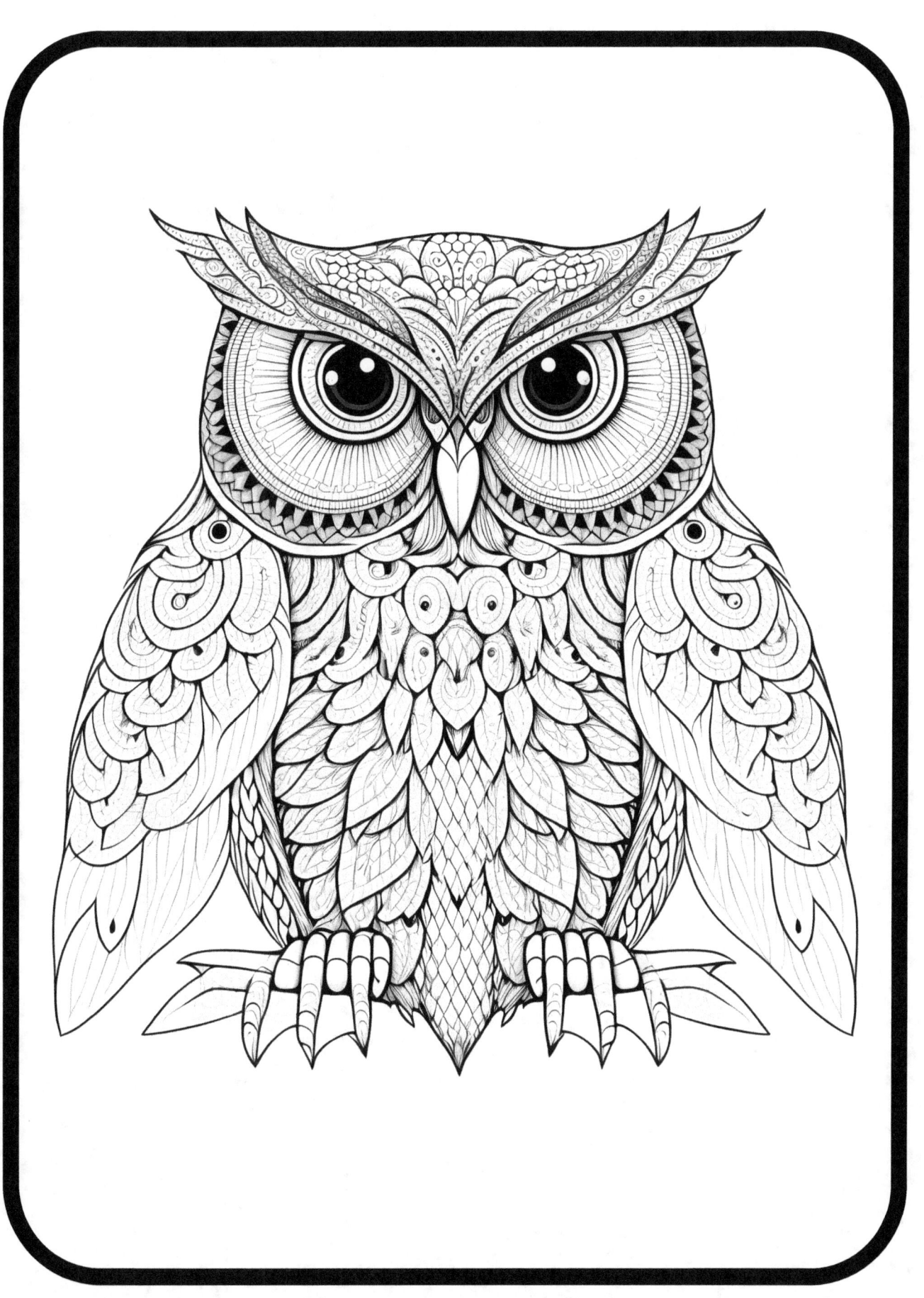

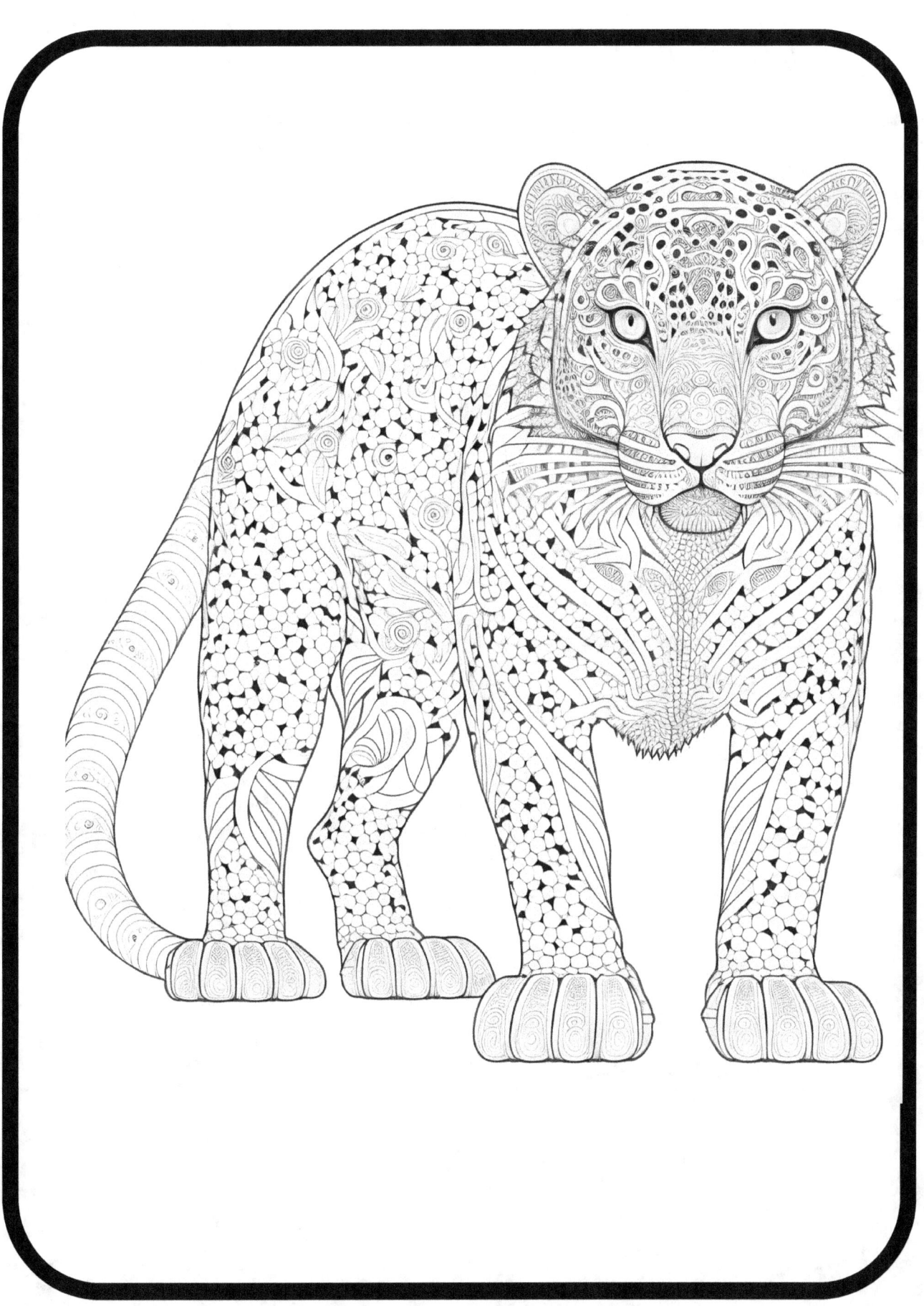

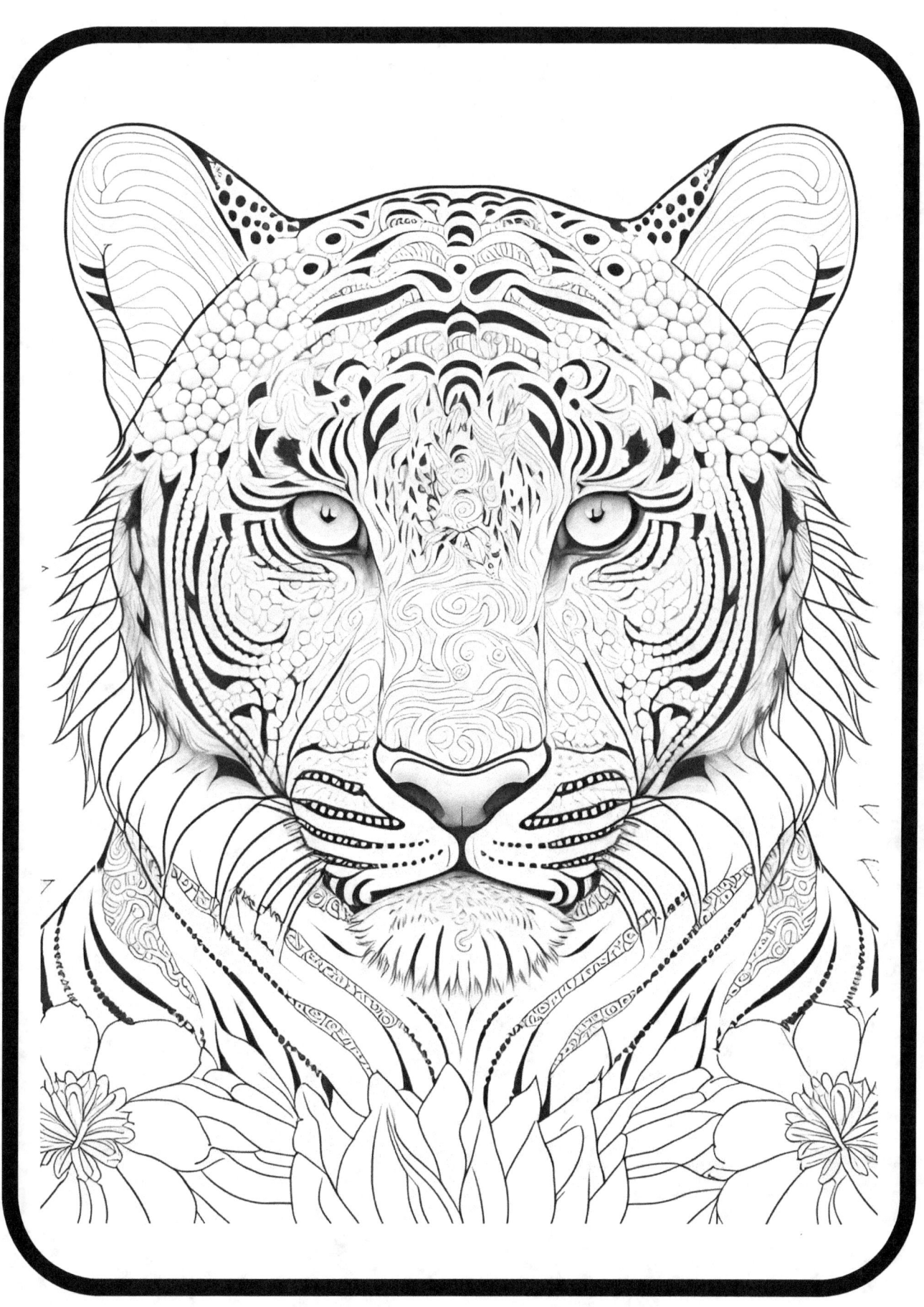

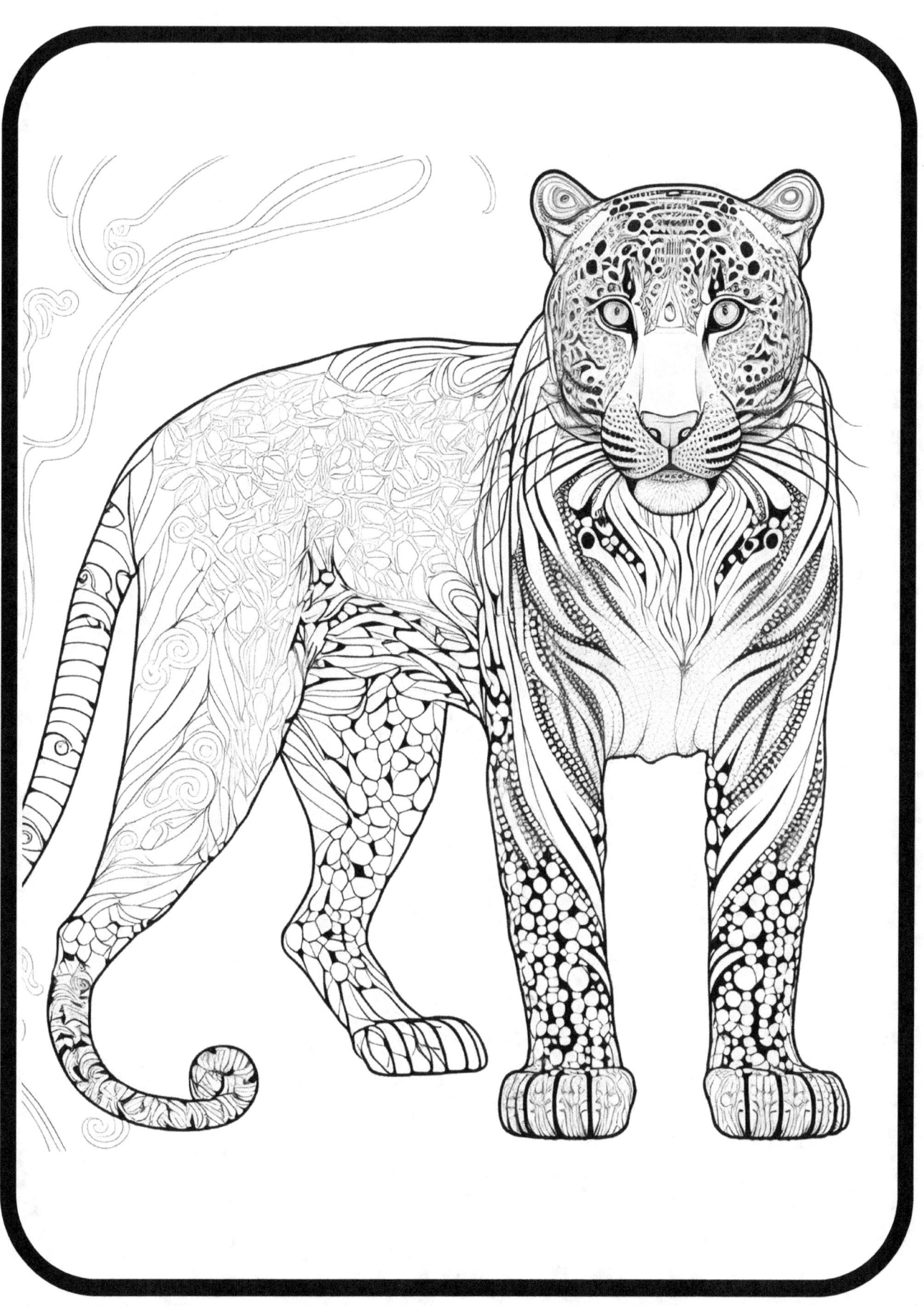

Find joy in the journey.

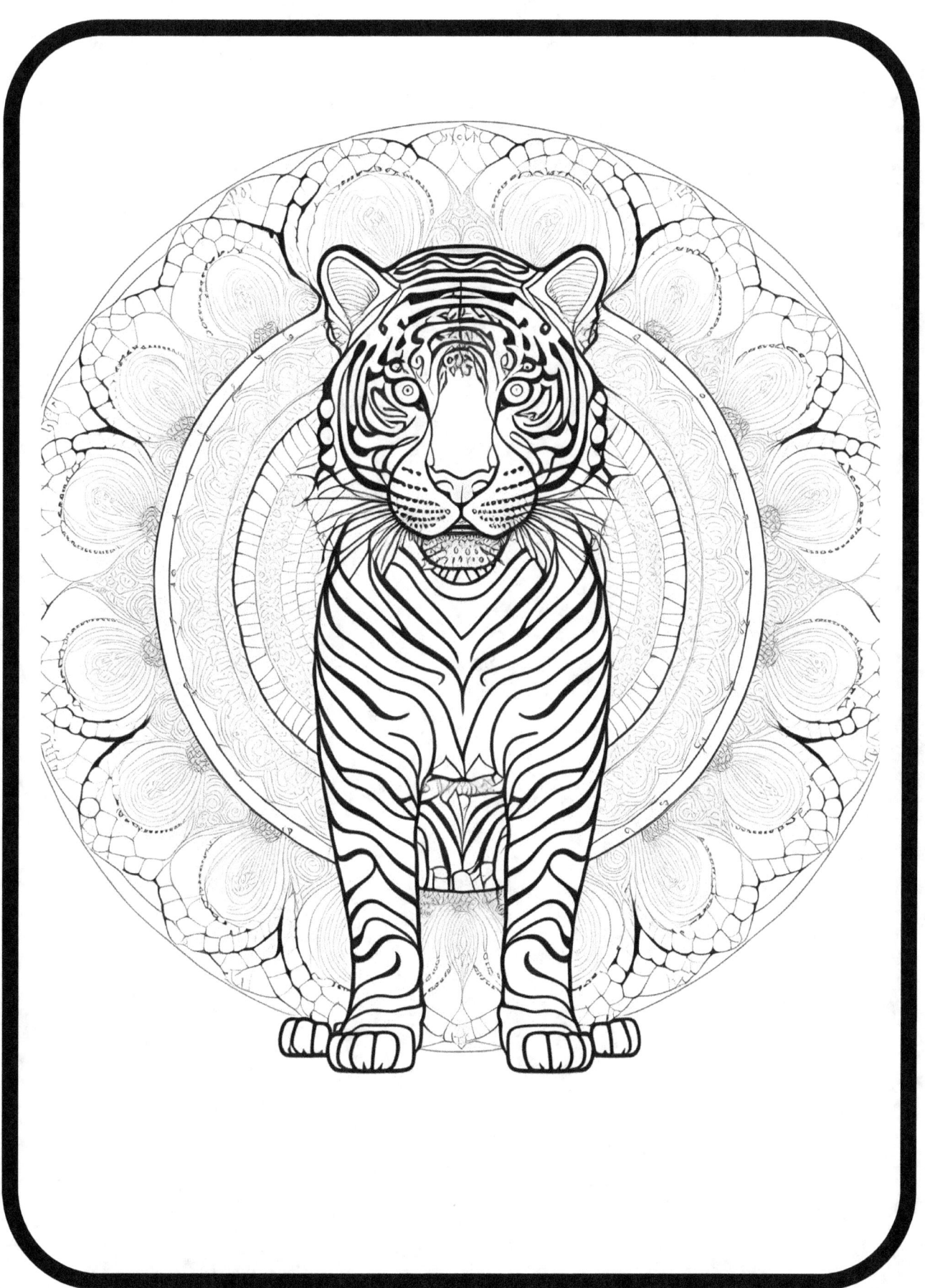

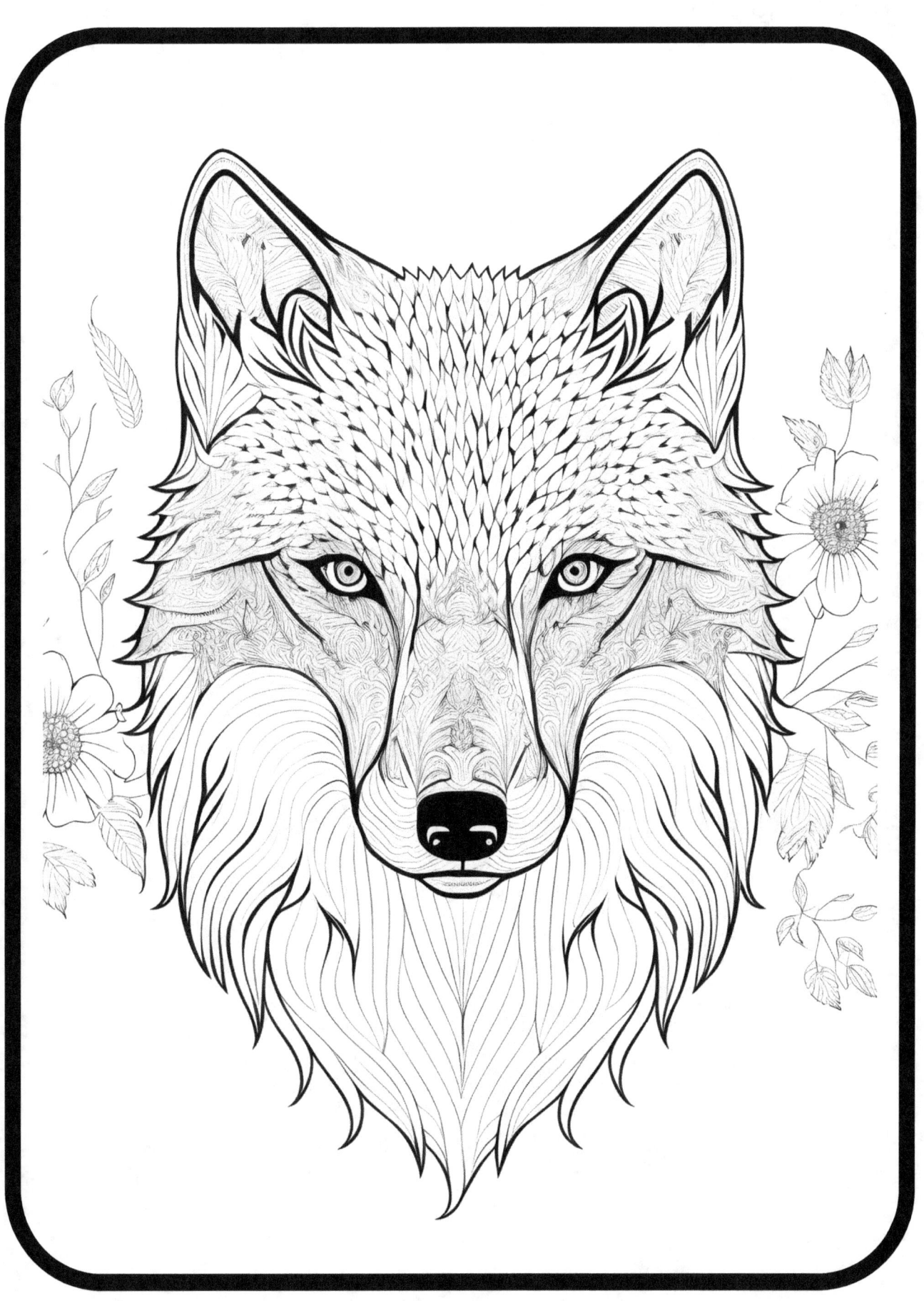

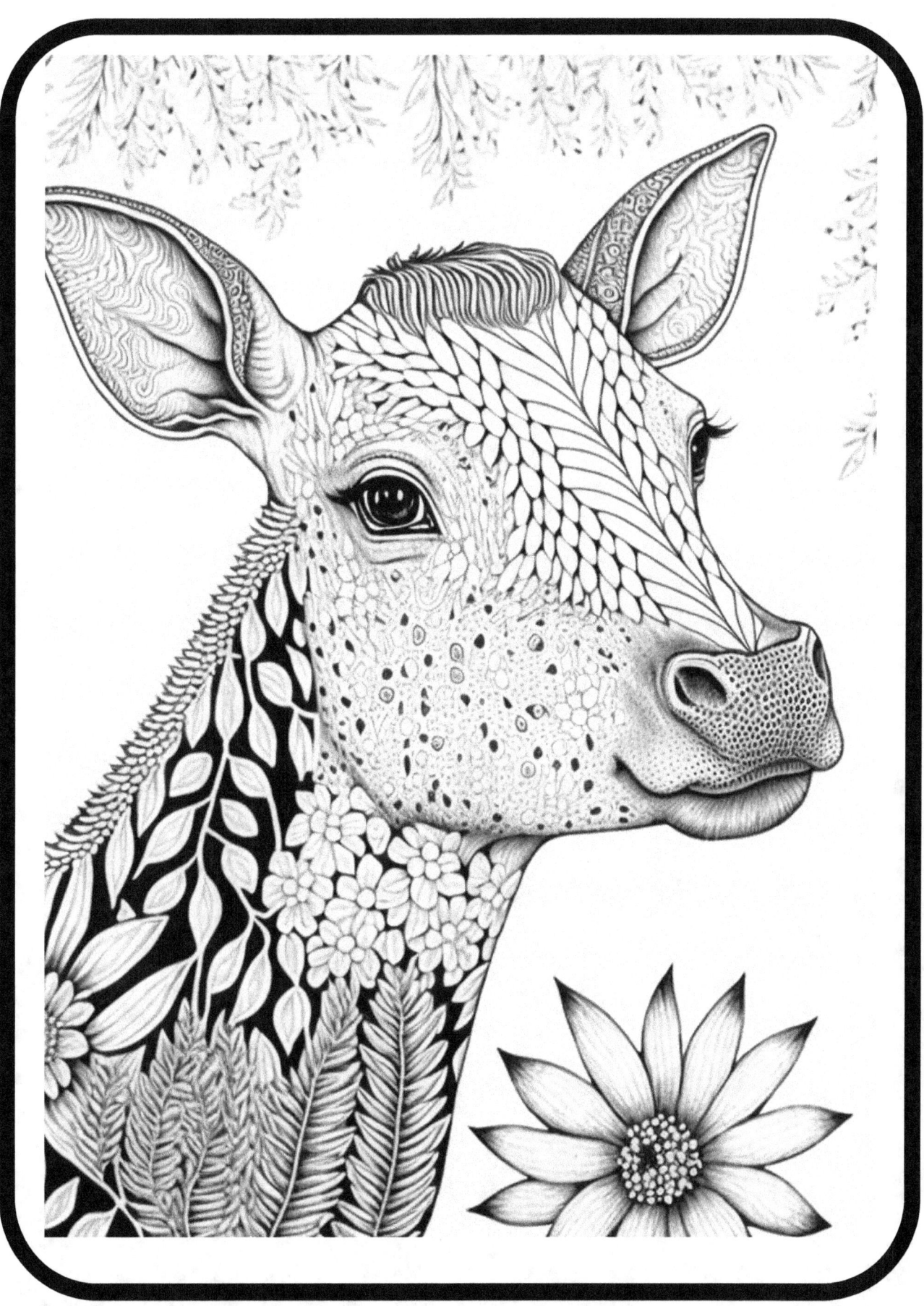

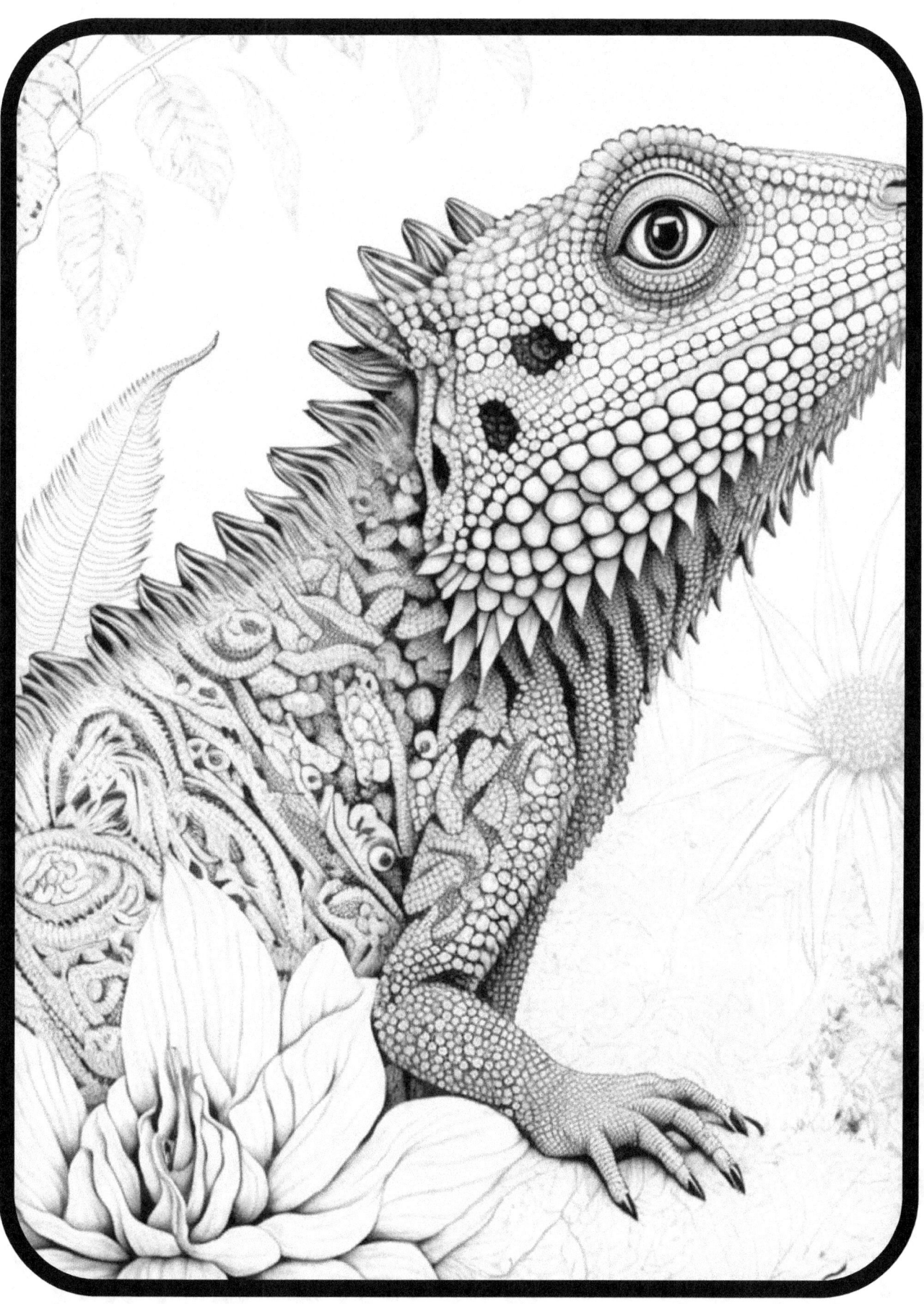

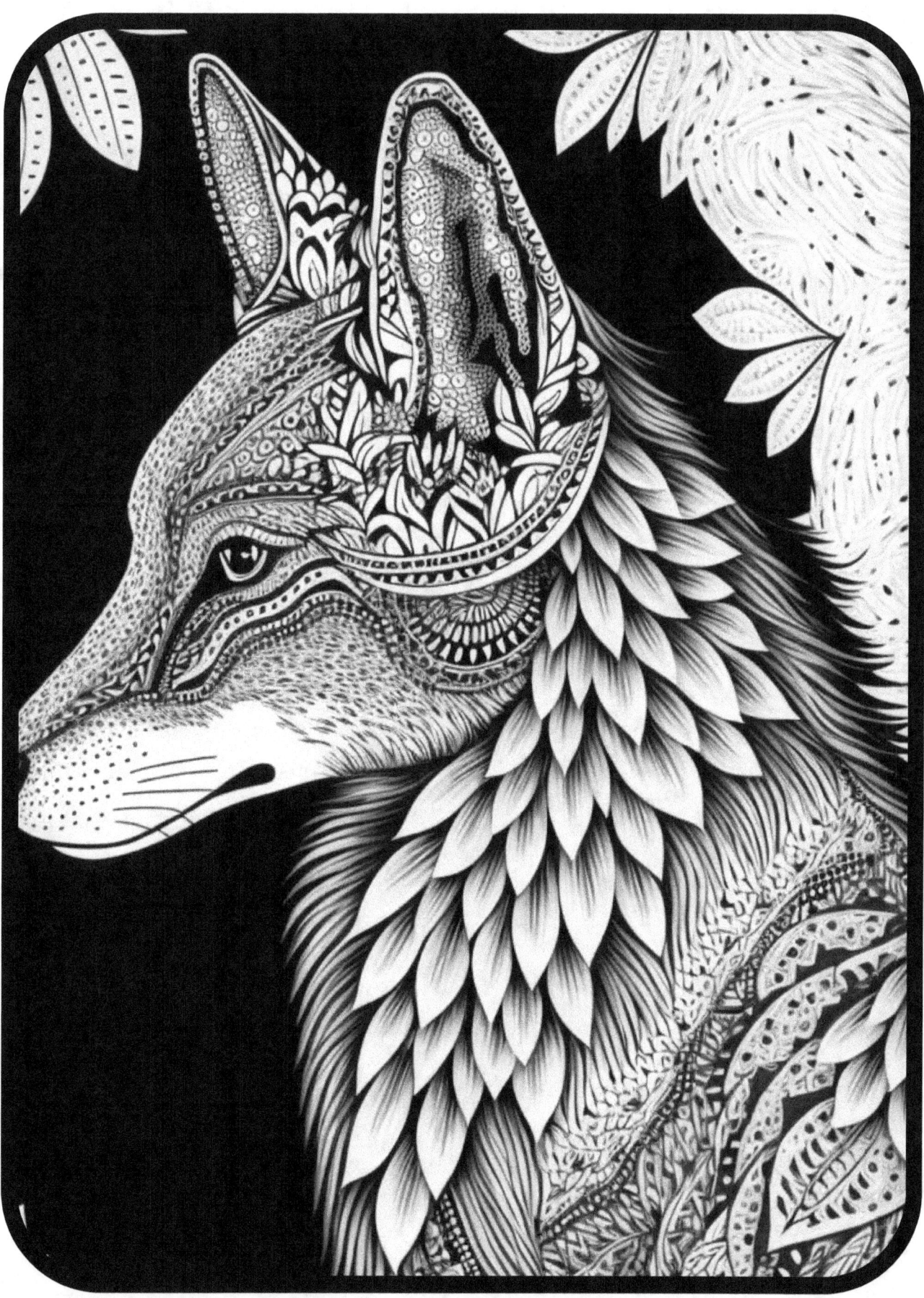

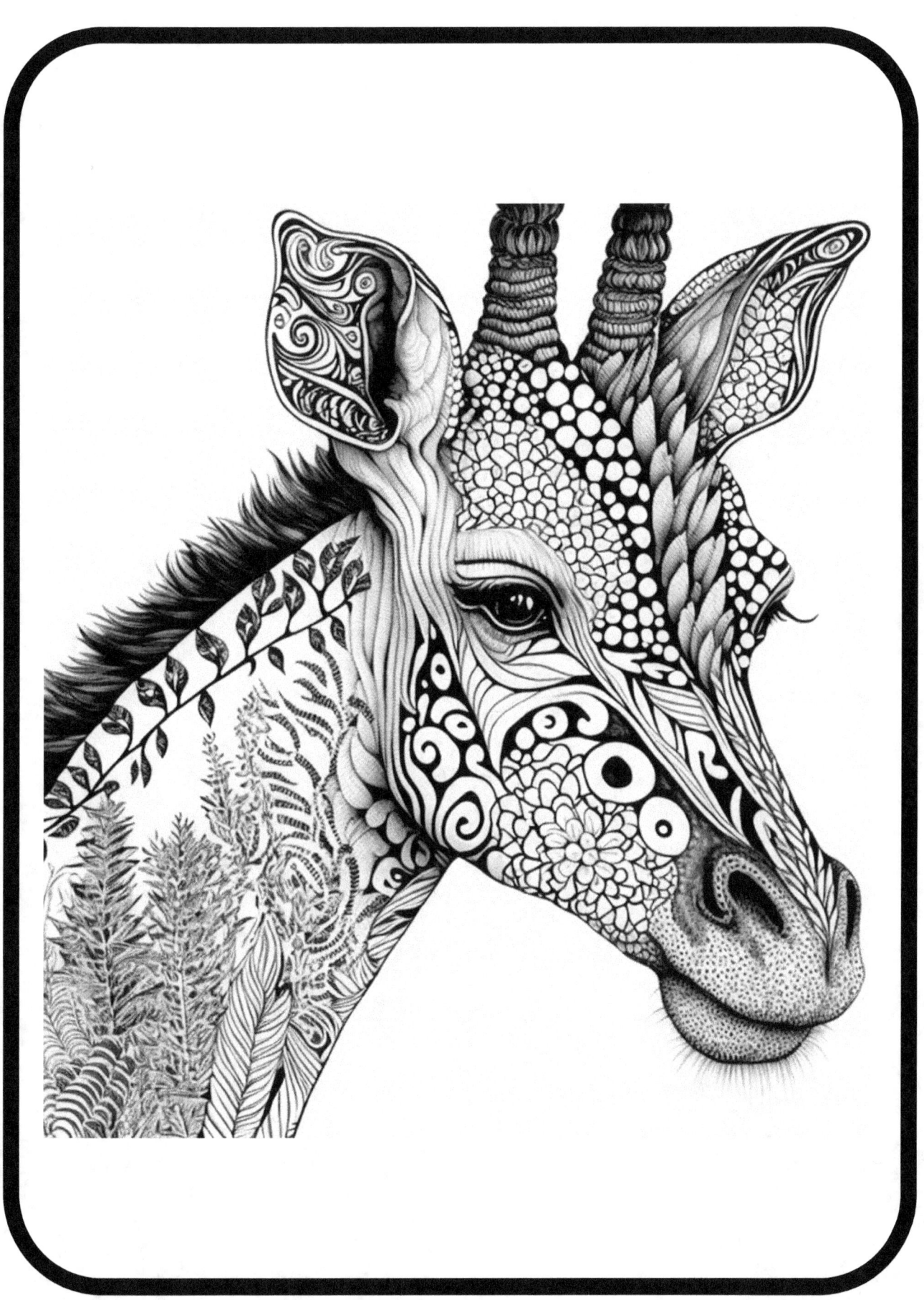

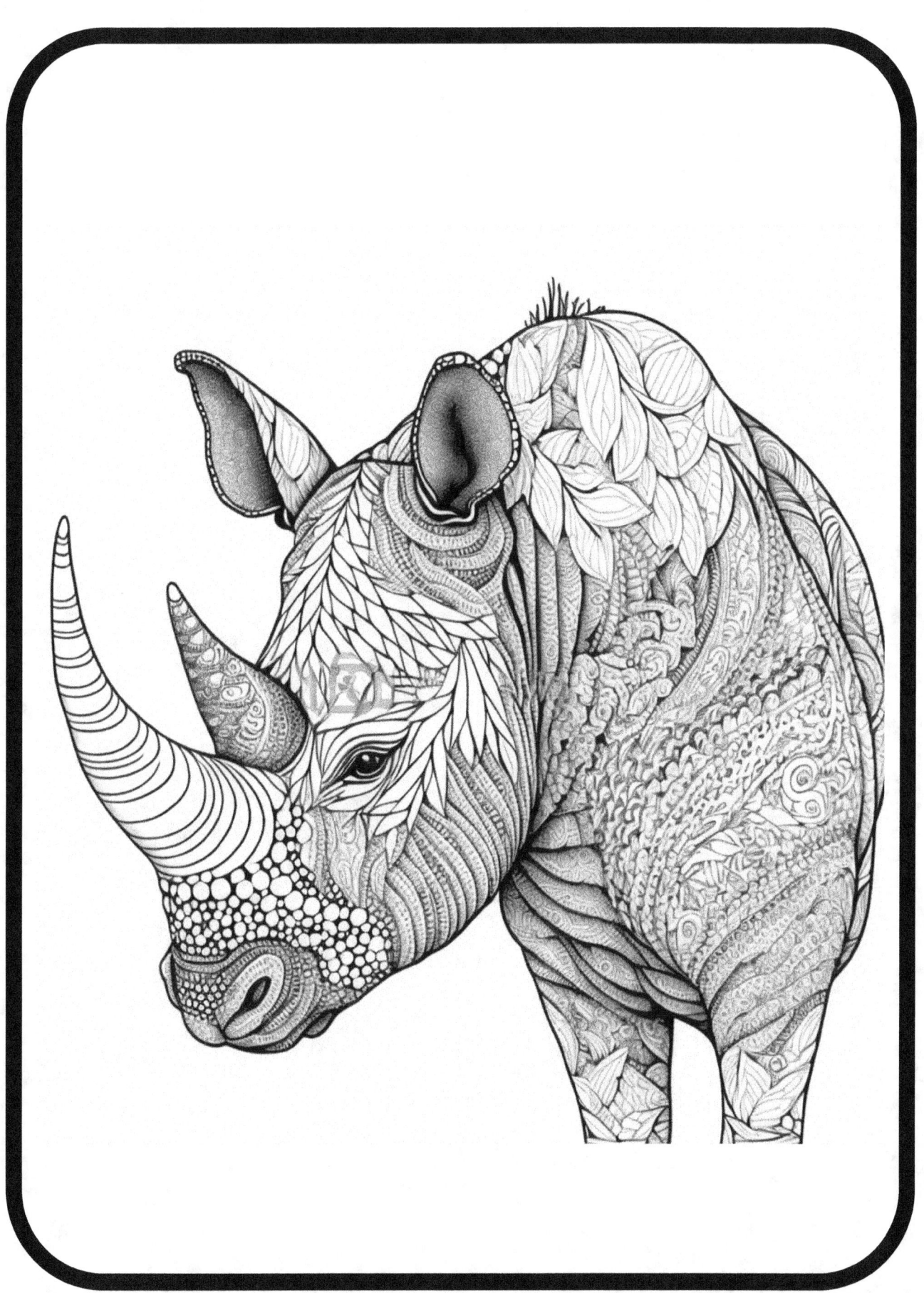

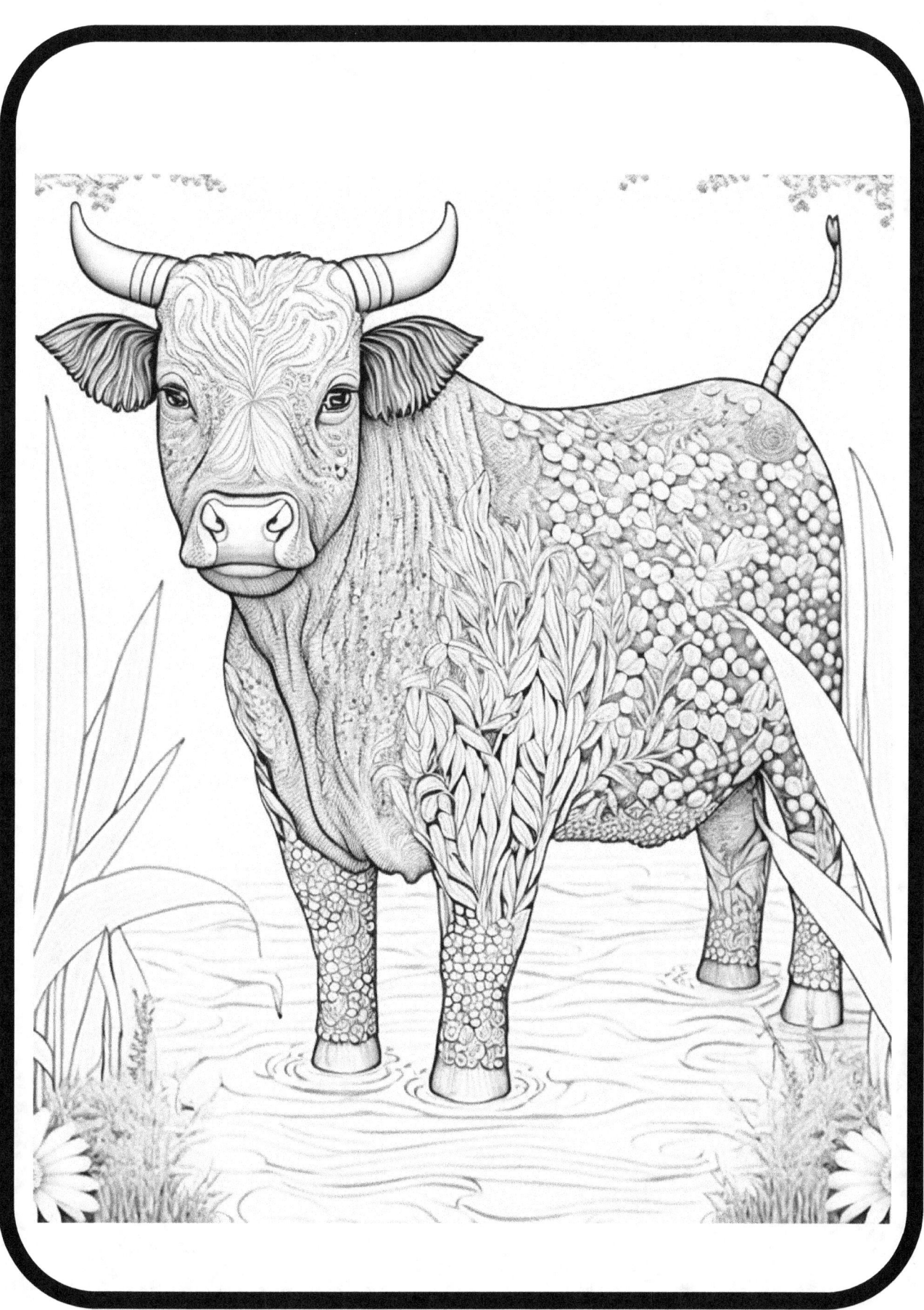

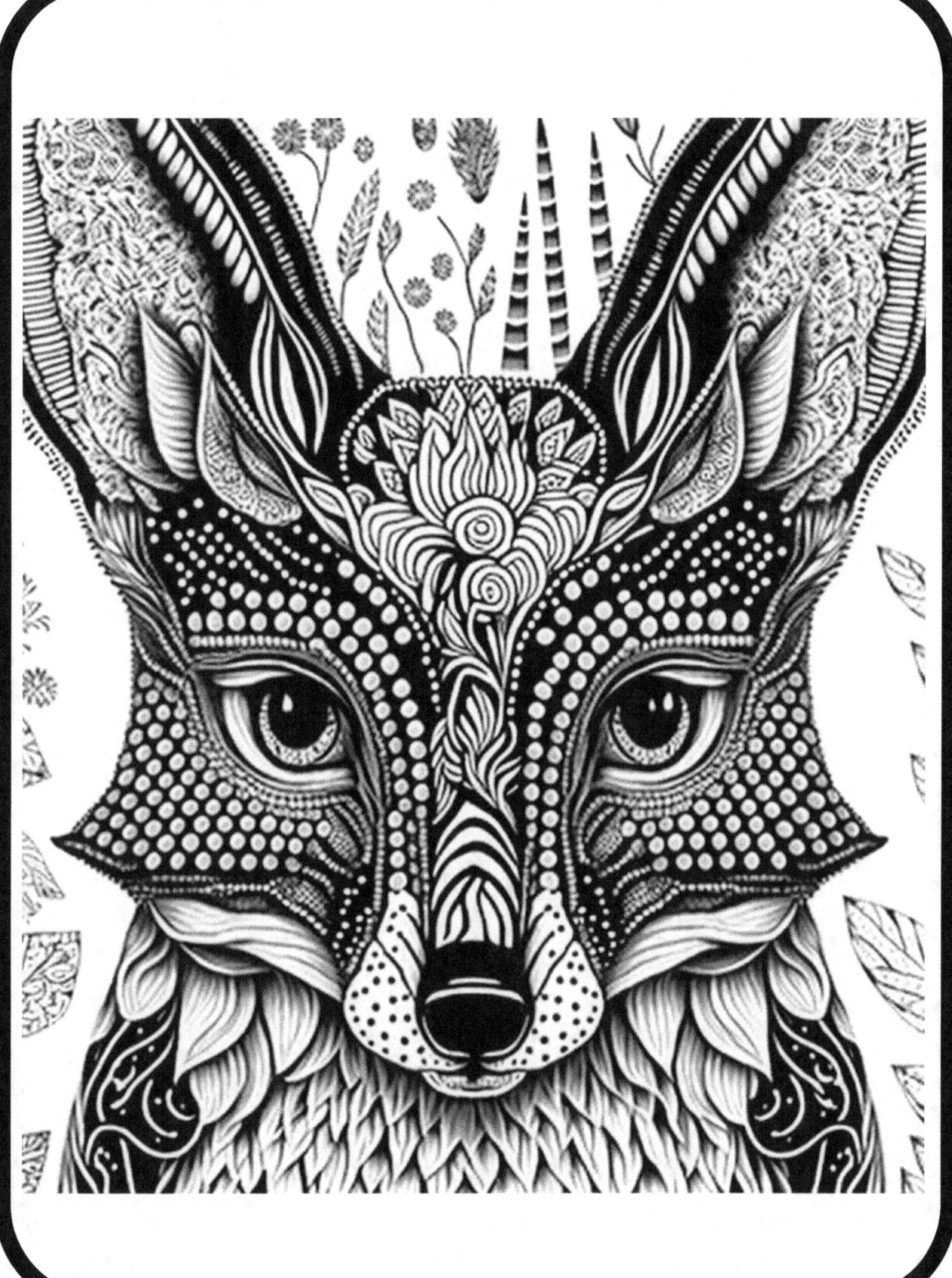

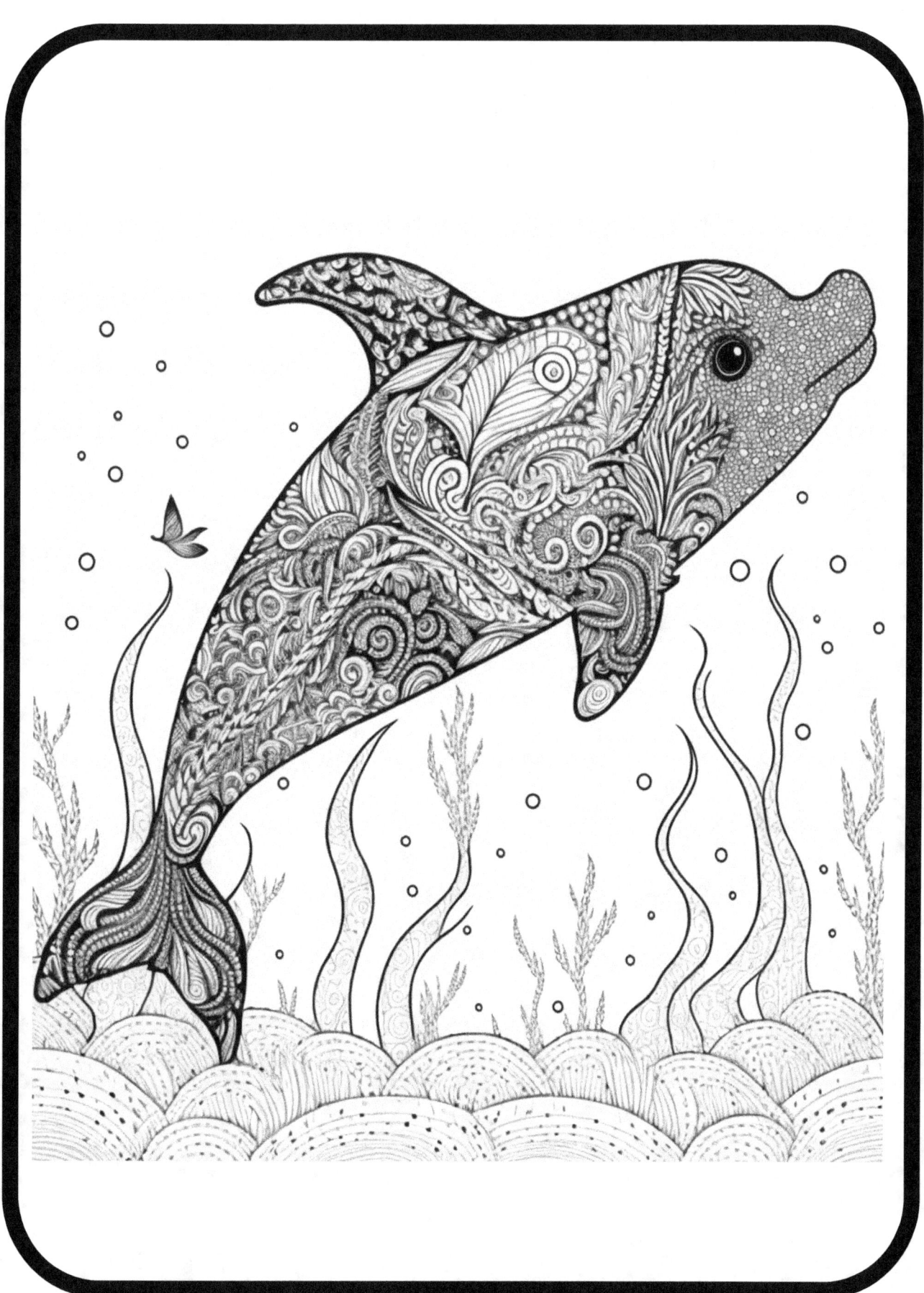

Stay focused on your goals.

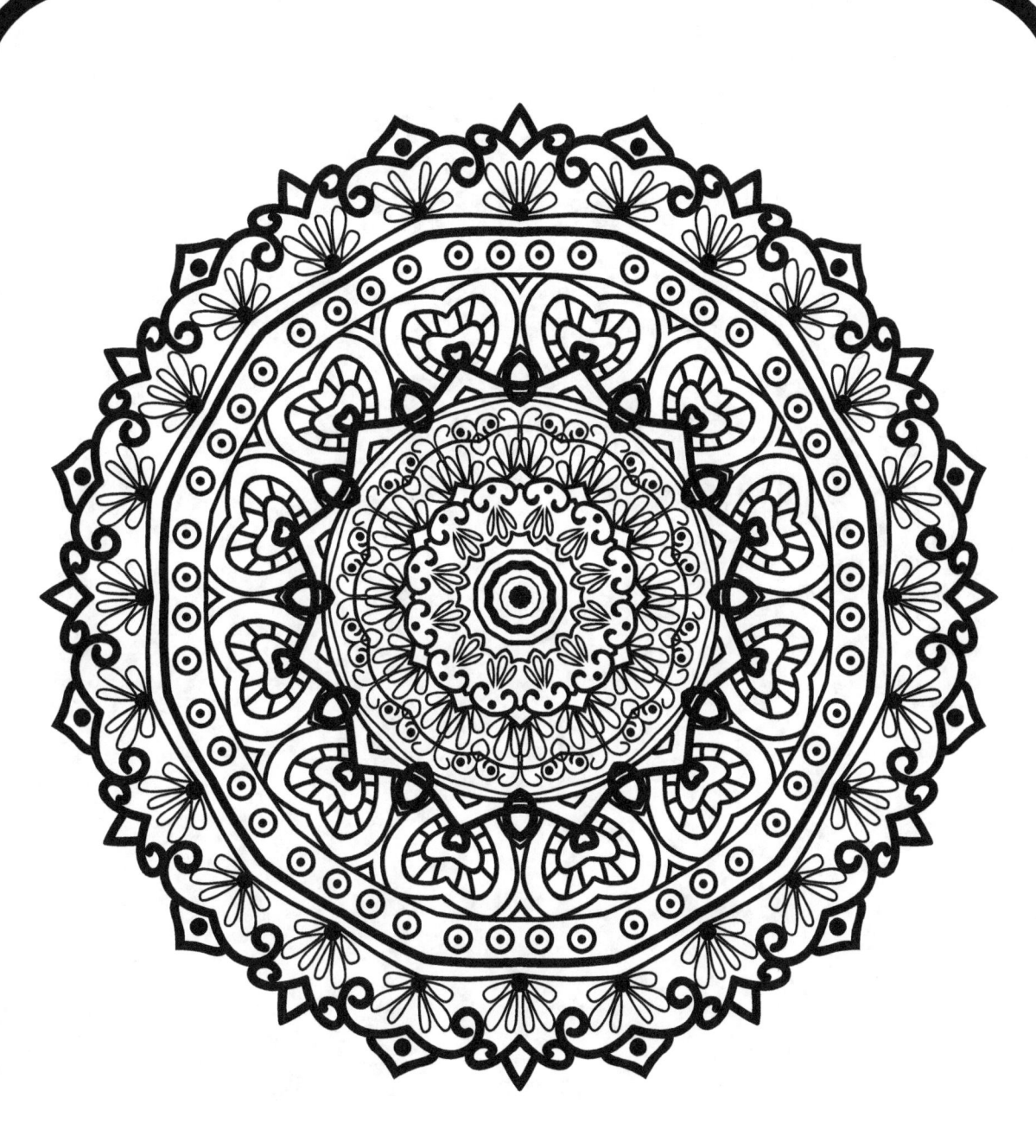

Thank you very much, I hope you enjoyed it as much as I did making it.

www.ingramcontent.com/pod-product-compliance
Lightning Source LLC
Chambersburg PA
CBHW081508220526
45467CB00010B/2835